THE TRANSNATIONAL "GOOD LIFE"

STUDIES IN LATIN AMERICA

The Studies in Latin America series features short works published by the Institute for the Study of the Americas at the University of North Carolina at Chapel Hill. Print editions are distributed by UNC Press and the UNC Chapel Hill Library hosts open access digital editions. The series promotes new scholarship on Latin America and the Caribbean focusing on the social sciences—principally anthropology, geography, history, political science, and sociology—and featuring diverse methodological approaches and perspectives on vital issues concerning Latin America and the Caribbean, past and present. For more information visit http://studiesinlatinamerica.lib.unc.edu/.

THE TRANSNATIONAL "GOOD LIFE"

Ecuadorian Social Clubs as Spaces of Resistance

Linda Jean Hall

INSTITUTE FOR THE STUDY OF THE AMERICAS
AT THE UNIVERSITY OF NORTH CAROLINA AT CHAPEL HILL

INSTITUTE FOR THE STUDY OF THE AMERICAS

This book was generously supported by the UNC Press Thomas W. Ross Fund
and the U.S. Department of Education Title VI National Resource Center funds.

Suggested citation: Hall, Linda Jean. *The Transnational "Good Life": Ecuadorian
Social Clubs as Spaces of Resistance*. Chapel Hill: Institute for the Study of the
Americas at the University of North Carolina at Chapel Hill, 2020.
DOI: https://doi.org/10.5149/9781469662510_Hall

Cataloging-in-Publication data for this title is available at the
Library of Congress, https://lccn.loc.gov/2020026492

ISBN 978-1-4696-6250-3 (pbk: alk. paper)
ISBN 978-1-4696-6251-0 (ebook)

Published by the Institute for the Study of the Americas
at the University of North Carolina at Chapel Hill

Distributed by the University of North Carolina Press
www.uncpress.org

Contents

Preface

While collecting data in Ecuador and three field sites in the United States between 2007 and 2016, I made a conscious effort to avoid research bias based on my lived experiences as a Black American citizen. The body of theory about the process of doing ethnographic fieldwork and writing from an outsider's perspective is frequently referred to as ethnography by an interloper or a person who becomes involved in a place in which they do not seem to belong. For this and other reasons listed below, this book more specifically is an exercise in what Bob Scholte (1981) and other prominent scholars (Davies, 1998; Ruby, 1982) describe as reflexive anthropology.

Reflexive ethnography represents an attempt on the part of the ethnographer to identify and explicate potential proclivities that may affect the entire spectrum of work required to complete a cultural study. One area in which the research could be accused of exercising bias relates to the way I see myself in relation to my U.S. citizenship. I view the world through a somewhat jaded lens, shaped by the experiences of my slave foreparents and reinforced on a daily basis by acts of discrimination and humiliation. Sociologists Sarah Mayorga-Gallo and Elizabeth Hordge-Freeman (2017) describe the apprehension felt by ethnographic researchers of color who actively concern themselves with issues of credibility— who worry about whether they will be seen as worthy of doing the research "because of being black," as well about the interviewees' passive perception of them—the way we will be perceived by the respondents as we work in the field (18). Early in the research I decided to forget about this troublesome dichotomy, and I moved forward as a well-informed researcher with good intentions and a willingness to listen, share my life experiences, and learn.

A second area of possible bias is that I do not share the egalitarian view that I am socially and politically a full member of American society (Marshall, 1950) by way of my birth in the United States. On the contrary, I am very cognizant of the fact that I occupy a marginalized space in U.S. society. At the same time, I bear all the responsibilities of citizenship. I am referring here to the seldom-researched national status of noncitizenship, the unfulfilled need to belong or, in the words of Nira Yuval-Davis (2006), the normal desire to participate and feel entitled to the benefits of being a citizen (198–199). Anthropologist Deborah A. Boehm (2011), in her nuanced analysis of the sense of belonging to the nation, concludes that it is a contingent membership in the state's citizenry, a "national membership that is partial, conditional, or relational" (161). My provisional status as a citizen—like that of the mostly naturalized Ecuadorians who contributed to this study—is inextricably and transnationally connected by way of genetic materials that originate and—from a transnational standpoint—span two continents. I argue that being a member of a group for which precariousness is the norm actually enables me to insightfully and compassionately work with a population undergoing the same type of uncertainty in reference to their status in the United States.

This active ethnographic study employed a mixed methodology and a multisited approach to explore the role of immigrant-founded social clubs as places of agency and success for the traditionally disenfranchised. According to Jean Schensul and Margaret LeCompte (2016), active research has the potential to equally benefit the researcher and key partners by bringing to the forefront new skill sets in data collection and distribution. In the spirit of Schensul and LeCompte, this ethnographic study is the result of "collaboration, community-based work, directional, designed participatory research, and an interaction between research and practice" (6).

Acknowledgments

This book stands firmly on the shoulders of a host of people who always believed I had the wherewithal to complete the long and personally exhausting mission of this ethnographic study. They are all prolific writers and highly regarded scholars. I want to be like them "when I grow up": Marc Becker, Christine Ward Gailey, Mary Hancock, Christopher McAuley, Yolanda Moses, Carmen Martínez Novo, Tom Patterson, and Howie Winant.

Also, a special note of thanks goes to my partners in this project, Gio Galarza and Monica Garneff, who patiently accepted all my calls and social media messages. By standing beside me since 2015—inside the classroom and out—you both, without hesitation, have enabled me to get to know your lives and your people.

Finally, I am eternally indebted to my son, Micah, for his moral encouragement and unfaltering support. Completion of this work was made possible because I am the benefactor of a wealth of familial support that includes that of a loving husband, Henry, and the members of my adoptive Harris-Cordero family in Ecuador.

In conclusion, this project and I were blessed! In Ecuador and the United States, Ecuadorians welcomed me and shared their experiences. I did this work out of a sense of admiration and deep love for a nation and people that embraced and continue to embrace me. ¡Viva Ecuador!

Abstract

The Transnational "Good Life" is an ethnographic study of the founding and maintenance of social organizations by emigrants from Ecuador in politically contested U.S. public spaces. By following in the footsteps of Du Bois (1900) who coined the term 'double consciousness', this book posits that racialization, an inherent characteristic of Global Apartheid, uniquely influenced the construction of complex Ecuadorian migrant identities in the U.S. The thematic focus is on the intersection of the empowerment produced in the social clubs with the desire of individual members to acquire the American Dream and the good life. This is an "anthropology of the good," (Ortner 2016) which brings to the forefront the lived experiences of immigrants claiming a high level of pre-migratory preparedness and success in the U.S. The Transnational "Good Life" is an analysis of evolving relationships within and outside the loosely connected network of Ecuadorian social clubs in the unique cultural milieus of Los Angeles, Miami, and New York City.

Introduction

"What do people make of place?" This question, which sparked Keith Basso's (1996, xviii) landmark study of Apache place-making, came to mind as I launched a new project on Ecuadorian migration in the United States. Place-making is a complex process involving the linking of past memories with the construction of new social identities. I undertook this exploration of Ecuadorian individuality as a transnational process after completing years of research in Ecuador from 2007 to early 2014. The findings formed a body of knowledge about the relationships in the Ecuadorian homeland among the nation's culturally multifarious populations. I began to build on these empirical data by asking a key question that would drive the project's research: In what ways does place-making in the settlement nation affect the practice of homeland-based norms and values?

The initial phase of the place-making project involved acquiring insightful testimonies from informants inside local Ecuadorian organizations in Los Angeles. A set of referrals eventually led to a crucial interview that provided the logic for analysis of issues framing this volume. The testimony of the subject referred to here only as "Anonymous" resulted in my seating this cross-national border project at the intersection of two bodies of theory: ideas about Latino diasporic immigration and the logic found in classic Afro-American analyses of transnational migrant marginalization. Afrocentric scholarship illuminates particular characteristics of individual identity bifurcation that is indigenous to the process of globalized migration. Also, the research findings and the circumstances leading to obtaining this informant's testimony support this study's central premise: there is a need to open new avenues of research about the formation of solidarity and cultural citizenship in Ecuadorian settlement community clubs. These organizations are rarely mentioned in previous scholarship despite having served for decades as domains of structural empowerment. In these community spaces, members and guests begin to aspire to achieve their own vision of success, including U.S. citizenship.

Anonymous began his session by listing his numerous professional accomplishments. He also expressed contentment based on a sense of himself as a transnational citizen who belongs to many nations. Trying to contextualize his current citizenship and ethnicity in terms of the descriptive categories in the 2010 U.S. census appeared to confuse him. He considers himself to be an ex-patriot of Ecuador who is self-tasked to acquire national identities and a vast network of professional connections across several European nations and the United States. "You don't have it here," he said, pointing to a copy of the racial and ethnic categories available in the census. "I'd say I'm Black Latino. I could be Afro-American, but I'm not., I'm not Afro-European. I'm American. I should be Afro-American, but I'm always seeing Black people here in America—when they do actually call themselves Afro-American, and you say, oh you're African, man, they deny that. . . . It's like you're confusing yourself. In Ecuador, I'm Afro-Ecuadorian. African is first when you say Afro-American." When he spoke of his citizenship status in other countries, he said that one reason he gravitated toward living in certain European nations was to avoid being racially quantified as a citizen. For him, in certain Euro-states his belonging depends only on his ability to exercise his talent, create an influential social network, and establish a lifestyle that reflects his membership in a successful class. Context is a central concern of this project, which asks how migrant points of homeland origin might affect their conceptualization of citizenship, professional mobility, socialization, and display of class membership.

To more closely examine the influence of context on the process of individuation, the study eventually included 25 key testimonies from project participants who represent the diverse ethnicities that characterize Ecuador's population along five major axes: 72% of the participants were mestizo (mixed Indigenous-White), 7% *montubio*, 7% Indigenous, 6% White, and 7% Afro. The empirical data acquired by doing field site research among members of Ecuadorian social clubs brought to the forefront the dynamic connections linking homeland ethnic difference, the development of membership solidarity, and the achievement of citizenship by many members. This analysis synthesizes the findings of the ethnographic study with theory to answer the following question: What factors define Ecuadorian ethnic diversity in the homeland and how do these cultural differences influence relationships and the attainment of positive social outcomes by club members?

Anonymous was far from the only subject of this study who found it difficult to self-identify according to the limited race and ethnic categories of the 2010 U.S. census. Several informants accused the population survey of ignoring and even trying to erase their existences. Those who did choose a category often justified their selection by giving it a meaning within the context of where they live in the United States. For example, "I'm White because here where I live in this country that means I have ancestors from Europe." In this way, the significance of racialized categories such as "White" and "Latino" are given a local meaning when attached to the acculturating body of the migrant. This ethnographic study is informed by my belief in the value of a multisited path to documenting Ecuadorian acculturation and identity formation as a dynamic phenomenon uniquely influenced by settlement social climates. For this reason, most of this study's subjects are long-time residents with strong economic, community, and in some cases political ties to one of three culturally diverse field site locations: Los Angeles, Miami, and New York City.

The majority of this project's subjects described themselves as living in an asymmetrical relationship between their former selves in Ecuador and who they have become in the United States. In a study of Ecuadorian migrant males and their south-central highland families, Jason Pribilsky (2007, 21) claims that "the value and meanings of family [*la familia*] had strengthened with migration." This ethnography examines Pribilsky's central thesis by bringing to the forefront the anxieties of migrants from culturally diverse Ecuadorian regions who acculturate outside the family and in sometimes multiple cultural domains. Acculturation in the context of this study refers to a process of adaptation in which migrants maintain a balance between the cultures of their homeland and settlement nations. The first sphere is one in which they shape who they believe they are today as members of communities that media scholar Joshua Meyrowitz (1985, 307) describes as collectives "with no sense of place." Because the social clubs have played a pivotal role as place-making sites in the settlement process of this population, the second space is the dynamic area of imagination—a "spacialized culture" (Low, 2016) in which they envision themselves as members or nonmembers of one of these organizations. The role of these social clubs in identity formation is only briefly discussed in Pribilsky's study. Their function is not even mentioned in the only other existing ethnography about Ecuadorian migration, by Ann Miles (2004).

Theoretical Foundations of Identity and Solidarity

The role of blood ties as a unifying agent in Black communities and in influencing the construction of Ecuadorian individual and organizational identities are both well-researched areas in ethnic studies. This blood-based characteristic that in classic Black theory Wade Nobles (1974) referred to as Africanity is the glue that held together communities for early twentieth-century migrating Afro-Americans (11). In fact, in the late 1970s sociologist Barry Wellman presented empirical findings that confirmed the vital role of kinship as Blacks extended these familial bonds to construct and network in grassroots social organizations. My research in Ecuador confirmed the claim by Alejandro Portes, Cristina Escobar, and Alexandria Walton Radford (2007, 244) that Latin Americans, like Black Americans, extended familial ties to establish local and transnational social organizations spanning the United States and their homelands. In both cases, contingent Afro and Latino citizens simultaneously formed mutually beneficial civil and social attachments to hereditary points of origin and settlement nations. This book explores a constantly changing phenomenon: the specific migratory experiences of Ecuadorians in the ways they claim success, citizenship, and belonging at the intersection of their founding and maintenance of a loosely connected network of U.S. social clubs.

At the beginning of my interview with Anonymous, he told me about his Afro-Ecuadorian ancestral background and his growing professional and familial global ties to the Euro zone and the United States. But he became visibly frustrated as he spoke about how each category in the U.S. census failed to accurately describe his unique identity: "I never see myself as a race, for me I'm a human being, a person. Even associating myself with the third space between where I was born in Ecuador and here in the United States would limit me." He described himself as successful in his industry of choice, a field in which he believes the stereotypes about his Black ancestry "gives me a way to overcome these ideas . . . and this absence of a category confirms that there is space . . . room for me to create an opportunity." In this narrative, the concept of place-making is the construction of what Homi Bhabha (1994) refers to as a junction during the process of acculturation where homeland and settlement ideas unite to produce new racial, gender, and class identities.

Post-1990s scholarship sheds light on reasons why some informants testified that at particular times in their lives they simultaneously embraced, rejected, and rebelled against their adoptive U.S. culture. For example, sociologist Eduardo Bonilla-Silva (2012) and immigration scholar and historian Mae Ngai (2014) posit that migrant Latin Americans construct their racial-ethnic identity based on the hegemonic Whiteness social model that defines U.S. society. The meticulous analysis of Tiffany Joseph (2015) confirms this assertion. Joseph also notes that the most salient qualifier of the racialized and global hegemonic social order constructed by the Brazilian immigrant population she studied is perceived phenotypical difference. Ecuador's most visible physical appearance is mestizo (~67% of the population is mixed Indigenous and White). My research found that anatomical characteristics are often overlooked in Ecuador in order to claim a genetic connection to the colonial or White-European past. The findings of this study directly correspond to Joseph's observation that migrants alter their perception of who they are, and they make a "transnational investment in whiteness" (145).

Expanding on the claim about Whiteness developed by Joseph opens the door to considering another finding of this research focusing on Ecuadorians: the unique positioning of Whiteness in the social hierarchies of each Latin American nation produces varying types of acculturation. Indeed, some of my Ecuadorian subjects expressed ambivalence in the ways they relate to and express Whiteness. For example, if they appear to be phenotypically White, the social context (i.e., in the workplace vs. family) often influenced their choice of racial identity. Phenotypical differences seldom resulted in social differentiation or hostility within families and between friends. In contrast, Whiteness mattered in the U.S. workplace and other professional environments because of the implied value of this status. An area in which my findings do not agree with Joseph has to do with the friendship choices Ecuadorians make in their personal lives. My close proximity over the years with Ecuadorian migrant individuals and families revealed that they—unlike Brazilian settlers—intermarry and establish relationships across all races and ethnicities. Ecuadorian social clubs host events that welcome and are attended by a cross-section of Latin American ethnic groups. Finally, because migrant Ecuadorians in two particular cases were very small populations in comparison to Mexicans, Puerto Ricans, Cubans, and so on, they frequently established mutually beneficial support networks at work and in their communities with Whites, Afro-Americans, Asian-Americans, and other Latin Americans. I found this to be true in the case of interviewees who were married to non-Ecuadorians and in many cases to Afro descendants from both the United States and other Latin American countries.

The interview with Anonymous concluded with his casting of migration as a dynamic and ongoing process. For him it is a journey in which he repeatedly crosses multiple national domains to accomplish personal goals and build distinct types of citizenship. "I have a green card here in the U.S. and dual citizenship in Spain and Ecuador and a house in which my mother lives in Barcelona.

I grew up in Guayaquil—but left at age 15 in 1998 to work all over South America. . . . I still don't speak English fluently. . . . But I made a future as a man from a country [Ecuador] in which my only options were to be a musician or athlete, or dead like so many of my friends. The only choices they had as men of a low class or poor class were bad." This focus on class led Anonymous to discuss the various ways he believed race, class, and gender influenced his development of global personas. "People can get lost no matter where they land. The same is true for everywhere I've been. I believe you must keep yourself. I never pretend." This book builds on his complex testimony to explore "keeping yourself."

"Keeping yourself" was a refrain I repeatedly heard during the two years of my research. Although many of the participants expressed this worldview differently, I began to understand the meaning of this recurring theme as a commitment to establish and/or maintain an identity that the individual believes to be positive and self-propelled. In this way, the immigrant informants claimed what anthropological theory refers to as the agency of a global actor (Kearney, 1995). At the same time, they couched their aspirations in their belief that despite achieving social and economic success for themselves and their families, they feel they are a part of the constantly growing and worldwide mass of disadvantaged migrants. Classic Afro-American theory, focusing on the creation of the Afro-American double consciousness, directly relates to the sociocultural disassociation experienced by migrant populations.

Ecuadorian Migrants from the Afro-American Perspective

The informants interviewed for this study all migrated between 1960 and 2010, a period during which U.S. immigration policies hardened with respect to populations from the southern hemisphere (Chavez, 2017; Abrego, 2014). The first phase of the research project resulted in the collection of empirical data based on participant observations and interviews during the final years of the Obama administration. Supplemental data obtained three years after the election of Donald Trump to the presidency (2016–2019) launch the first chapter's historical analysis of the push factors that influenced Ecuadorian migration. The time frame of the project, spanning two diametrically opposed presidencies, resulted in the documentation of a growing feeling of hopelessness in many of the study's subjects. This rising sense of foreboding was first captured in the final interview with a 70-year-old at the end of 2015, a year before Donald Trump's election. She expressed a deep sense of dread that after 30 years of naturalization the election of Trump would lead to her deportation. Feelings of impending eviction and un-want or estrangement are examined in great depth in Afro-American studies. Early 20th-century scholarship in Black studies explores the marginalized status of the global migrant from within the context of the Afro-American experience. In assessing the value and function of the otherness of a global or two-sided identity, this project embraces the description by W. E. B. Du Bois (1989, 3) of a socioeconomic and highly emotional state of double consciousness—"this sense of always looking at one's self through the eyes of others, of measuring one's soul by the tape of a world that looks on in amused contempt and pity."

According to Du Bois, within the American hegemonic domain the exploited masses are rendered powerless and invisible. This research posits that accompanying this erasure is the creation of a double sense of self and a perception of a type of essential or realistic experience in which there is opportunity to choose to succeed or fail despite the stigma of double consciousness. The testimonies in this book speak from a double consciousness—a shared identity of those with blood ties that situate them on the wrong side of what Du Bois (1989, 30) referred to as the "color-line,—the relation of the darker to the lighter races of men." John E. Wideman (1990, xiii), in his introduction to the Vintage Press edition of Du Bois's classic *The Souls of Black Folk*, expands on this idea, taking into consideration the growth of a globalized labor force comprised of peoples of African, Asian, and nonexclusively White descent: "DuBois' insights have profoundly altered the way we look at ourselves. . . . He locates us, sketches our features, gives us names. 'Us' turns out to be most people on the earth, people of color, emigrants, refugees, mixed bloods, exiles, the poor and dispossessed, women and men who didn't count, who were unseen and unheard." Wideman evokes Du Boisian logic to explain the negative outcomes of migration. My research explores another side of this same experience by concentrating on Ecuadorian migrants who claim to have attained success as a result of immigration to the United States in spite of being positioned on the "other" side of the color line.

Embracing a Du Boisian perspective does not imply I stand in opposition to the vast theoretical body of knowledge that claims migration by double-consciousness individuals is a painful and debasing process. Yes, the history of those on the other side of the color line is littered with the bodies of the forever "dispossessed" (Boehm, 2016)—the undocumented, traumatized, and overly incarcerated individuals who emigrated to the United States from Latin American countries. But this study's empirical data, in the form of witness testimonies fused with the logic of Wideman, demonstrate that there is room in the corpus of immigration scholarship to ask a question about the exercise of agency by what Du Bois and Wideman describe as the powerless global double identity: What kinds of choices and opportunities affect dual-identity individuals as they construct good and bad migratory outcomes?

Du Bois's concept of racialized double consciousness served as a lens to analyze a set of data acquired between 2015 to 2017 about the lived acculturation experiences of Ecuadorian migrants. The study captured their feelings of uncertainty and possible displacement due to a rising tide of anti-immigrant sentiment in the United States. This sense of instability contrasted with the personal and collective achievements they claimed. For the subjects of this study, the social climate in which they achieved these successes was framed by both the profit-motivated and quasinationalistic American Dream (Stoll, 2009) and the desire to establish a more simplistic good life.

Anthropologist Michael Lambek (2010, 1) defines the good life as a service-oriented sense of "freedom, judgement, responsibility, dignity, self-fashioning, care, empathy, character, virtue, reasoning, justice, and the good life for humanity." A symbiosis during acculturation of these two value systems is a part of transnational identity construction, a process that begins in the homeland.

The Ecuadorian state has been and continues to be a political structure conducive to the formation of new racially defined hierarchies (Rahier, 2008; de la Torre, 2018). In the racialized space of Ecuador, institutions have traditionally been divided along lines of both culture and class (Lamphere, 1992). This has made the nation a hegemonic actor that differentially exercises power over the bodies of individuals. In this way, the state frames and shapes the life experiences of Ecuadorians. For centuries, events and various powerful ideologies have influenced the identity construction of Ecuador's multigenerational migrating population. This dynamic is well-documented in the sociological studies of Carlos de la Torre (2010), Brad Jokisch and David Kyle (2008), and anthropologist O. Hugo Benavides (2004). These scholars provide evidence that oligarchs and/or the government purposefully created ethnic and class divisions that at times rapidly and cruelly defined individual citizenship. In response, during the 20th and 21st centuries historically disadvantaged citizens have attempted unsuccessfully to achieve national sociopolitical equality. This is especially true for the Indigenous and Afro-Ecuadorians, whose physical features and cultural practices were repeatedly used to justify their societal marginalization.

Table 1.   Ethnic Population According to Population Censuses

Ethnic Population of Ecuador According to Population Censuses	How is ethnicity counted?	Indigenous (Percentage of Population)	Afro-Ecuadorians (Percentage of Population)	*Montubios* (Percentage of Population)
1950	Language	16.3		
1962	Not counted			
1974	Not counted			
1982	Not counted			
1990	Language	3.84		
2001	Self-identification	6.83	4.97	
2010	Self-identification	7.0	7.2	7.4

Figure 1. The above summary of Ecuadorian census data is an official summary of the disbursement of ethnic groups in Ecuador from 1950 to 2010 (Novo, 2009).

	Ethnic group	2007	2008	2009
Poverty measured by income				
	Indigenous	62,5%	65,9%	68,2%
	White	30,9%	25,7%	26,3%
	Mestizo	33,0%	31,4%	32,7%
	Afro-Ecuadorian	50,6%	43,4%	42,9%
	NATIONAL	36,7%	35,1%	36,0%
Underemployment Index				
	Indigenous	68,5%	73,0%	68,5%
	White	51,2%	46,6%	49,1%
	Mestizo	52,8%	52,0%	54,6%
	Afro-Ecuadorian	56,4%	58,8%	61,6%
	Other	75,9%	65,8%	63,8%
	NATIONAL	53,5%	52,6%	54,8%
Urban Unemployment				
	Indigenous	3,6%	3,7%	3,5%
	White	7,0%	9,4%	8,5%
	Mestizo	5,9%	7,2%	7,8%
	Afro-Ecuadorian	8,9%	7,6%	11,7%
	Other	5,2%	11,1%	0,0%
	NATIONAL	6,1%	7,3%	7,9%
Property of Housing				
	Indigenous	75,6%	75,9%	79,8%
	White	65,2%	65,4%	65,0%
	Mestizo	65,3%	67,4%	64,7%
	Afro-Ecuadorian	62,9%	64,7%	65,1%
	NATIONAL	65,9%	67,7%	65,7%
High School Education				
	Indigenous	3,4%	5,3%	7,8%
	White	16,2%	19,9%	25,4%
	Mestizo	18,7%	20,3%	21,3%
	Afro-Ecuadorian	6,9%	10,7%	9,8%
	NATIONAL	17,0%	18,7%	20,1%
Illiteracy				
	Indigenous	26,6%	25,8%	24,9%
	White	5,1%	5,3%	4,7%
	Mestizo	6,7%	6,3%	6,8%
	Afro-Ecuadorian	9,2%	8,3%	7,3%
	NATIONAL	7,9%	7,6%	7,8%
College Education				
	Indigenous	4,2%	4,2%	4,2%
	White	8,5%	8,5%	8,4%
	Mestizo	9,2%	9,3%	9,8%
	Afro-Ecuadorian	7,0%	6,9%	7,3%
	NATIONAL	7,9%	7,6%	7,8%

Figure 2. Social indicators by ethnicity in Ecuador (Sánchez, 2012).

The case of Ecuadorians actually claiming Afro ancestry exemplifies the ways a racial-ethnic isolationism based on differences in physical traits and cultural heritage functions in Ecuador. Geneticist César Paz-y-Miño stunned the Ecuadorian nation by publishing the findings of a multiethnic study verifying that ~96% of all Ecuadorians have genomic ties to African ancestry (Paz-y-Miño, Guillen Sacoto, & Leone, 2016). However, when asked by the national 2010 national census to ethnically self-identify, only little over 7% of the Ecuadorian population of 14.4 million categorized themselves as being of African or Afro-Ecuadorian heritage (Figure 1 Ecuadorian Census). The sources of this conflicted identity are issues of race and ethnicity that come to the surface when viewed objectively.

Carlos de la Torre and Jhon Antón Sánchez (2012) meticulously extrapolated the socioeconomic indicators for the entire Ecuadorian population to reveal how this plays out in real life. Figure 2 Ecuadorian Ethnicity depicts the disproportionate distribution of economic resources and the effect of reduced educational achievement closely tied to ethnic identity.

The exception to the above demographics is the population of approximately 50,000 *montubio* farming families. *Montubios*, whose territorial region in Ecuador is in the hinterlands of the port city of Guayaquil, refer to themselves as "Indigenous/Black/White" or triethnic. There is little social science research about *montubios*, but Karem Roitman (2008) claims that what sets them apart is their viewpoint on the value of Afro ancestry, which has turned preconceived notions about Afro heritage in Ecuador on their head. In 2001, *montubios* exercised collective power to petition and receive recognition from the state as an ethnic-racial identity based on their unique mixed heritage and shared exercise of particular cultural practices. In this way, *montubios* established themselves as a *pueblo*, or distinct ethnic-political identity—a status that the state also granted in legislation to Indigenous and Afro-Ecuadorians during the 1990s. The *montubios* in Ecuador proudly display and politically capitalize on their African heritage (1-3). In this study, the transnational experiences of two *montubio* subjects reveal how the racialization process in the United States favoring Whiteness undercuts *montubio* migrants' claim to Blackness. The interviews with the *montubios* opened the door to explore characteristics of Latin America's and Ecuador's most ubiquitous operative population concept and categorization: *mestizaje*.

Mestizaje

Many scholars have shown that the heterogeneous structure of Ecuadorian society today continues to be divided along lines of implicit differences in skin color, class, and gender. These ideas about difference are firmly seated in the colonial regime or rule of caste, the *regimen de castas* (Hollenstein, 2009). Other prominent researchers add that it is important to additionally analyze the politics of *mestizaje*. *Mestizaje* is a social stratification practice that socially marginalizes Blackness and Indianness in favor of a national Indian-White identity (Strawn, 2009). Ecuador, like many Latin American nations, embraced and politicized *mestizaje* during the 20th century. Even though *mestizaje* is an ignoble notion, the legitimization of this practice by the state exacerbated the marginalization of specific underrepresented populations, especially Indigenous and Afro descendants. In this study, homeland characteristics based on regional, ethnic, and phenotypical differences in ethnic groups are shown to be a factor that determined social club membership and the relationships among these organizations. Also, within these clubs the administrative functions often defied traditional beliefs that favored male leadership. *Mestizaje* intersects in Ecuador with other insidious traditional praxes including machismo.

Machismo

Machismo is a systematic practice found in all institutions of Ecuadorian society. In the United States, pragmatic Ecuadorian migrants challenged to achieve both the American Dream and a good life often found it necessary to minimize machismo's impact on their double-consciousness identity and social club mission construction. Interdisciplinary literature about machismo in Latin America describes its characteristics as the victimization of women, the internalization of trauma by children, and the social degradation of males perceived to be weak or less masculine. Sociologist Raewyn Connell (1995) claims that there are different types of masculinities indigenous to Latin America: (1) competing hegemonic masculinities that each in different ways practice domination and (2) alternative masculinities. Nonhegemonic machismo is exercised by men with limited power, that is, male members of ethnic minorities and poor classes. Imbalances in Ecuador that reflect the impact of machismo exist in the family, the community, and state institutions.

This research builds on the anthropological argument by Matthew Gutmann and Mara Viveros (2004, 114) that context is also important in the practice of machismo. An analysis of hegemonic masculinity from this standpoint must take into consideration geographical location as well as the related uneven distribution of power inherent to the practice of misogyny. Two previous studies of Ecuadorian immigration to the United States by Pribilsky (2007) and Miles (2004) provide empirical evidence that the elevation of the female role in the transnational job market results in a reduction or even the elimination of the male practice of dominance in the home and community. According to Miles (2004), it is unfair to portray all Ecuadorian women as susceptible and submissive partners to the propagation of machismo. Her research in Ecuador found many examples of noncompliance (46). This study expands existing knowledge about machismo as a transnational and malleable practice with two findings: (1) machismo can also affect relationships between genders across national borders, and (2) transnational power dynamics favoring females have often diminished the role of machismo in the family and community.

Due to the frequent economic crises in Ecuador, family patriarchs lost control of businesses and the marketplace. This disruption also resulted in a decrease in both wages for men and the demand for highly qualified male craftsmen. Scores of Ecuadorian men were emasculated by this downturn, finding themselves unable to provide for their families. Some of the witness testimonies in this research pointed to the tendency of male partners to abandon their traditional roles as the head of the family when confronted with extreme economic insecurity. The transnational jobs in small offices and factories that did exist during these turbulent times preferred to employ women. As a result, thousands of Ecuadorian women entered the international workforce. Several of this study's female informants spoke with pride about the first time they stepped out of their customary duties as child nurturers and managers of the home to take on greater financial responsibilities. Their comprehensive and insightful testimonies support findings by historian Brian Gratton (2007) that many such women also assumed the lead role in planning the family's future outside Ecuador. This study also engages other scholarship, including that of Alexandra Espinosa, Luís Horna, Rodrigo Mendieta Muñoz, and Nicola Pontarollo (2019), who assert that "Ecuadorians have a weak interaction with the natives of the host country." Based on the testimony of multiple informants, Espinosa et al. (2019, 53) found that Ecuadorian settlement in the United States had the potential to benefit from the migrants' creation of supportive and interethnic social networks.

Despite the promise of opportunity, immigration to the United States has always been a complex and dangerous process. The journeys of this study's subjects happened between 1960 and 2010, a time in U.S. history marked by an increase in illegal entries and the tightening of immigration laws. To navigate these obstacles, the female subjects of this study first constructed a transnational network of friends and family already established in the United States, into whose homes the women often planned to move without their husbands. When the circumstances in the United States supported migration, they made the journey with their children to find jobs through this same network. In this way, the women facilitated the migration process on both ends. Several of the women in this study who were most victimized by machismo left on their own with little hope of seeing again the children and the abusive partner they left behind. Others meticulously crafted an extensive and often multi-year plan with the objective of reuniting the family in the United

States. Although *mestizaje* shaped and framed the lives of the migrants in this study in Ecuador, the transnational reordering of the woman's role in this paradigm frequently resulted in a reduction of this debasing and demoralizing practice across global spaces.

Highlands versus Sierra

Even today within the social domain of the Ecuadorian nation, there are malicious stereotypes and unfounded claims that people born on the coast are crude, effeminate, and prone to lascivious behavior. Conversely, in part because the seat of Spanish colonial and postrevolutionary governance has always been in the highlands, many coastal Ecuadorians respond to the belittling taunts of highlanders by claiming that people from the mountainous region are too formal, haughty, and arrogant. Visual and textual narratives successfully normalized the contentious binary relationship in Ecuador between regions and hegemonic masculinity. Allan Charles Dawson (2014) refers to this as a psychological phenomenon (10–11) at the individual level, and Audrey Smedley (1998) and Jennifer Crocker and Brenda Major (1989) assert it is also emblematic of the way stigma functions across various social groups within a shared geographical domain. This research confirmed that the regional animosity between the coast and the sierra influenced Ecuadorian immigrant relationships in the United States.

In addition to such qualitative ideas about *mestizaje*, machismo, and regional stereotypes, a previous study by Ecuadorian economist Mónica Mancheno (2010) sheds a quantitative light on the intersectionality, or junction, of race, gender, and class that has shaped the acculturation of Ecuadorian migrants. Mancheno claims that in 2006, 58% of these migrants to various global locations originated in one of three provinces: Guayas (Guayaquil), Pichincha (Quito), and Azuay (Cuenca). The statistics from 2006 reveal that the migrant population of highlanders that year was ~3% higher than that of immigrants from the coastal zone. Migration from predominately Afro and Indigenous populations was less than 5%. The subjects of this study were from all three regions and tended to seek out and associate with Ecuadorians with whom they shared class and cultural backgrounds endemic to these regions.

Mancheno also explores various socioeconomic characteristics of migrant Ecuadorians, and her findings concur with those of Miles (2004) and Pribilsky (2007): migrants to the United States from Ecuador until the 1990s were usually male. This research reveals that much can be learned about their acculturations by fine-tuning this approach to consider the role of migrating and well-prepared women. The subjects I interviewed brought to the surface a supporting narrative, showing that many times these women were the first to both migrate and obtain employment outside of the informal sector in the settlement nation. Nancy Foner (2001), in her ethnography about immigrants in New York, observed that in the competitive and ethnically diverse U.S. social domain many immigrants of all ethnicities arrive well-educated, well-funded, and educationally equipped to compete in U.S. society. When discussing preparedness for migration, it was common for the subjects of this study to shed light on the findings of both Mancheno (2010) and Foner (2001). The shared opinion of these scholars is that preparedness is directly attached to the acquisition of social capital—familiar and community networks of support—a concept Latinx feminist theorists define as the "complex relationship of commitment and trust" (Fitts & McClure, 2015). Embracing the need to establish trust, this project extends to interviewees some degree of confidentiality by referring to these well-known public figures by using only their first names.

The interviewees also confirmed that they feel there is a close relationship between preparedness and success. For example, informants believed that having a high level of education and/or a marketable trade skill enabled them to resist the ultimate failure, a penniless return to Ecuador. Each spoke of never doubting that their Ecuadorian educations and training were valuable transnational assets qualifying them to achieve the American Dream. Although the participants in this study envisioned the American Dream as a goal, previous scholarship about Ecuadorian migration by subjects with varying skill sets suggests that not all Ecuadorian migrants to the United States aspire to achieve this specific economic ideal (Pribilsky, 2007). Oswaldo, then president of one of the social clubs we will examine, succinctly described the confusion and sacrifices often associated with achieving the American Dream. In 1969, he arrived in New York City with a degree in psychology and the dream of becoming a college professor. He immediately began to establish a network of friends, including an Argentinian and other Ecuadorians, who helped him as he searched for work and improved his English. Oswaldo described these relationships as ones in which he experienced belonging and support: "All were dedicated to learning and self-improvement. . . . Plus, we formed a sports club and I was appointed in 1972 as president. Today, I still serve as secretary, and the club has members from all over the city. Part of the American Dream is to obtain property—unlike renting—to own you can use the property for your own purposes—in order to make one's ability to achieve, to improve oneself" (Oswaldo, 2016). The first 10 years in NYC, Oswaldo dreamed of moving back to Ecuador. Although the property Oswaldo owns includes a house in his home nation, he listened to the advice of his friendship network that cautioned him that by moving back to the Ecuador he would stifle his chances to advance his education and lose all the benefits he gained by living in the United States.

In almost every case, subjects interviewed for this study described the American Dream as a lifestyle full of hard work toward citizenship and economic opportunities. The advantages included owning a house and a reliable car, having a secure job, and being able to support the educational advancement of their children. This study uses a more nuanced lens to evaluate a claim that success is rarely possible in the United States for Ecuadorian migrants. Gustavo López (2015) found that Ecuadorian immigrants earn less than other Hispanic groups, while the percentage of them living below the poverty line is higher than for the United States' population as a whole. This project proceeds from the assumption that acculturation in the United States is a cross-gender experience involving individual constructions of attitudes and beliefs about what constitutes failure and success. In an era of surging job insecurity in the

United States, success itself has taken on different meanings for the double-consciousness identity.

Leonor, an informant who had lived in New York City for decades, took issue with a core concept of success in the United States, the American Dream. Although she feels she has effectively changed socioeconomic class membership because of her naturalization and dual citizenship, she still finds it necessary to stand in opposition to "the American way." For example, she expressed concern with what she referred to as a (North) American lack of empathy for transnational workers. She resists this dynamic by overseeing a training program designed to incentivize and vocationally prepare migrant students to compete in New York City's garment industry. Despite being highly motivated, she added that her students are aspiring to achieve an unattainable goal, success in a field ravaged by offshoring and wage reductions. Leonor described the garment industry as comprised of transnational entities controlled by capitalists who exploit a mostly non-White labor force whose achievement is irrevocably curtailed by the regime of racialization. Her comments suggest what geographer Andrew Burridge (2014, 466) would describe as a post-neoliberal system characterized by "a lottery of birth" favoring the rich.

According to Leonor, "The American Dream changed my life, all my family is here, and although I have a little home in Ecuador, something I can say is mine there, I now want to stay here in the United States with my family because I am not sure I could be happy in Ecuador" (Leonor, 2016). Her home in Manhattan is an apartment now threatened by gentrification. Even though she may be forced to move, she stated that as a woman of her age— over 30—she knew that a return to her homeland to resettle was no longer possible. She described the current chaos and instability of employment in Ecuador, which includes mass firings and age discrimination. All these are factors that she feels would prevent her from attaining her current dream of a good and contented life. For the subjects of this study, the lure of achieving the American Dream was always present in their minds, working in tandem with Ecuador's socioeconomic and political instability to ground their settlement. Their lives were dictated by an ever-present fear of a penniless return to Ecuador and a push back into the bottomless pit of the transnational migratory stream.

Chapter Organization

The malleability of a double-consciousness lifestyle comes to the forefront in chapter 1, which examines Ecuadorian migration both historically and contextually. Ecuadorian immigrants discuss traditional worldviews from Ecuador and how these are challenged by English-only educational standards and the process of embodiment in the three field site locations: Los Angeles, Miami, and New York City. Embodiment is the "mental activity [that] is fundamentally and intrinsically rooted in the body's interaction with the outer world" (O'Connor, 2017). These discussions about bodily existential experiences prompted the subjects to discuss issues of contemporary interest, including their relationships with other ethnic groups, and the conflation of all Latin Americans into racialized categories, such as Mexican, Hispanic, and Latino. Being Ecuadorian within the context of varying Latin American and multinational/ethnic social hierarchies in each of the three locations relates to the conjoining of ideas from the homeland and settlement nations about class and achievement. The immigrants' viewpoints shine a light on the value of factors such as lighter skin color, the formation of community unity, and the acquirement of legal citizenship.

The approach of the chapters that follow is to focus on the identity construction of individual Ecuadorian migrants and call attention to how this process shapes their sense of belonging. Each case study quarries the basic premise that a sense of belonging for Ecuadorian migrants is related to their ability to exercise professional mobility, establish effective social networks, and attain membership in a successful class. This study does not claim that these are the only characteristics marking place-making. However, the exploratory analyses bring to the surface personal conflicts with ideas I have already discussed about human difference that transcend global boundaries and shape individual settlement. In this way, each subject defines what "keeping yourself" means—a declaration of selfhood that contradicts the gross misconception that Latin Americans are a threat to the American ethos because they are incapable of assimilating. Empirical evidence emerges in the testimonies to support a counterargument based on the ontological divide: a sense of belonging or alienation. The informants' claims support the humanitarian opinion held by anthropologists who are deeply immersed in their communities of study: successful integration into U.S. society by Latin Americans often leads to the higher achievement of acculturation—an amalgamation of homeland and settlement-nation cultures that is of value to both societies.

The next three chapters highlight the social clubs: Club Ancón in Los Angeles; Vecinos en Acción, a family pantry and outreach organization in Miami; Liga, also in Miami; and the Ecuadorian Civic Committee Nueva York in the Queens neighborhood of Corona. As we will see, the demands of the social climates in each location have unique impacts on Ecuadorian organizational relationships. Commonalities also emerge regarding success. For example, as many of the subjects achieve the American Dream, they cling to the related idea that anyone can pull themselves up by their bootstraps. Lorraine Hansberry (1959) questioned the bootstrapping ideology from the standpoint of the historically marginalized in her play *A Raisin in the Sun*, as did Latinx scholar Lisa Cacho (2012) in her exposé about the criminalization of the unprotected and racialized in U.S. society. In this study, a second-generation Miamian disavows the bootstrap narrative while an independently wealthy Californian strongly advocates the notion as being his key to success. Rather than critique the questionable ethos of hard work that epitomizes the American Dream, this study brings to the surface the possibility that the quest and achievement of this ideal for many migrants facilitates the creation of social organizations promoting cultural citizenship.

During the 2014–2015 phase of research in the three cities, the organizations of focus shared a common problem: decreasing membership. Each social club addressed this issue differently and each performed altruistic services globally and locally. Most of these associations sponsor events at their facilities. At the time of the first phase of research, each in some way supported or participated in citywide Ecuadorian and Latin American celebrations. For example, Ecuadorian social clubs in Los Angeles encourage entrepreneurial ventures that stimulate the growth of an increasing number of Ecuadorian-owned businesses. Unfortunately, the majority of the organizations have not developed programs to support the undocumented. Classic Afro-American scholarship about the noncommittal attitudes of successful members of Afro-diasporic populations provides insight into the behavior of affluent and highly educated elitist migrants of other multiethnic diasporic and double-consciousness movements. The findings of this study add weight to Paul Gilroy's (1993) claim that it is common for more successful diasporic elites to avoid uplift activities for two reasons. First, having achieved some level of cultural citizenship, many who have attained prestige and success embrace a sense of entitlement that walls them off from members of the diaspora who they feel are not like them. Second, some elites cling to ideas such as bootstrapping that are deeply embedded in the individualism of "occidental modernity" (34).

Throughout all phases of this study, there continued to be a need to help fellow immigrants, a struggling class of both long-term and new arrivals, to acculturate and seek opportunities in the United States. Often, club policies created massive obstacles. For example, membership in the associations is often based on Ecuadorian geographical and familial ties. I mentioned this issue as a potential problem to several club administrators. The association board members politely listened but did not respond as I suggested that such criteria, based on class differences, favor the settled while delegitimizing and alienating the undocumented. This study also found another circumstance that is rapidly limiting organizational growth in all three locations. In each site, the arrival of Ecuadorian migrants is decreasing, while the populations unqualified by birth to join the clubs are sharply increasing. The latter include intraracial and international partners of Ecuadorian natives and an increasing number of multiracial and multinational children.

The three chapters about the social clubs discuss many of the factors like club membership that characterize Ecuadorian acculturation in the United States. Each brings into focus one of the elements of place-making, or the construction of a sense of belonging. Chapter 2 foregrounds the impact of racialization on the creation of social networks in Los Angeles. Chapter 3 examines the free exercise of personal and professional social mobility in Miami. Finally, in chapter 4, Pribilsky's observation about the impact of class differences among Ecuadorian migrants provides a backdrop to a discussion about existing and future models of Ecuadorian service organizations in New York City. Changes in club missions constituted the primary area of focus during the 2019 final phase of research for this study.

In late 2019 interviews, the subjects continued to provide revealing updates about the local social climates and the current status of their organizations. They discussed the election of Donald Trump as U.S. president and the impact of increasing xenophobic nationalism and related draconian immigration policies on the clubs' visions of community service and organizational growth. The findings of the final phase of research support a claim that directly relates to the future of Ecuadorian social clubs in the United States: the exercise of mobility as a community organization, the construction of strong social networks, and the establishment of multiethnic club memberships have the potential to produce positive outcomes for these critical associations.

Anthropologist Sherry Ortner (2016) inspired this study in urging us to go beyond the boundaries of "dark anthropology." An ethnography of darkness emphasizes the harsh and brutal dimensions of negative structural and historical conditions that produce human oppression and suffering. Ortner broadens what at the time of her article's publication was a ubiquitous and exclusive focus by ethnographers on gloomy social outcomes. Ortner recommends that researchers look beyond the obscurity of the human condition. I embrace Ortner's suggestion by examining the migration of Ecuadorians as their production of cultural citizenship. The positive elements of cultural citizenship I explore in the chapters that follow includes place-making, or what is known as the construction of a sense of belonging. The concept of selfhood came to the surface as this project examined the creation in a particular space—Ecuadorian social clubs—of an identity reflecting a dedication to service, sound judgment, dignity, empathy, and sociopolitical justice. In this study, Ecuadorian migration to the United States is shown to be a positive and successful experience that religious anthropologist Michael Lambek (2010) would describe as an anthropology of good. This work reveals positive choices made within the context of a double-consciousness migrant identity. For this reason, I asked participants to contextualize, expose, and discuss themes including "freedom, judgement, responsibility, dignity, self-fashioning, care, empathy, character, virtue, truth, reasoning, justice, and the good life for humanity" (59).

The cautionary scholarship of Lars Rodseth (2017, 408), in his Ortner critique titled *Hegemonic Concepts of Culture: The Checkered History of Dark Anthropology*, challenges scholars to employ a lens reflecting "a synthesis of light and dark . . . as good anthropology has always sought to do." In the first three chapters, a dual focus on the light and dark elucidates the hegemonic power dynamics and organizational leadership compromises encountered during Ecuadorian migrant settlement inside and outside their social organizations. An analysis of the changes in club structure and place-making compiled in 2019 brings to the surface the plasticity of the double-consciousness identity.

In July 2019, I conducted telephone interviews with club administrators to update the status of clubs in New York City and Miami. These testimonies came at a chaotic time in U.S. history. Immigrants—documented and undocumented—lived in fear of possible roundups by U.S. Immigration and Customs Enforcement (ICE). The rules governing amnesty suddenly and illogically changed, narrowing the avenue for legal immigration, especially for Latin Americans. This campaign of terror and the separation of children from their parents at the U.S. southern border continued unabated despite the best counterefforts in the courts by groups such as the American Civil Liberties Union. Los Angeles subject Yolanda's deepest fear became reality as the line between citizen and noncitizen moved in a direction that no longer favored naturalization. Despite the rising uncertainty, the Ecuadorian social clubs in 2019 were aggressively engaged in a higher level of community uplift.

One indicator of progress is the recruitment of younger members. In 2019, the New York–based organization was creating part-time paying jobs for youth. The club was also hosting internships to support recent college graduates and helping graduate students to secure grant funding for programs hosted by the organization. Members were enthusiastic about the future of the club because of their burgeoning efforts to create a more accessible and service-oriented public identity. Steps they were taking included developing a digitally connected modern network. Through this internet presence they have increased their mobility and visibility within the community by decreasing the time it takes them to respond to local needs. Another benefit produced through a wider internet exposure is a heightening of the organization's social capital by constructing more direct links to political agents, high schools, universities, and colleges.

As further evidence that outside forces have a limited impact on membership and event participation, the "Don't ask, don't tell" club guideline of the Miami association is now relaxed to include mixed families and what the club identifies as non-Hispanics. In 2015, policies for membership in the club required the applicant be born in Ecuador, but in 2019 they were changed to no longer demand Ecuadorian birth. Over the past three years, the Miami club administrators have also made considerable efforts to attract corporate sponsorships. Outcomes of the discussions between board members and local businesses have resulted in the donation of expensive medical equipment and other resources to support relief efforts in Ecuador. Although the club does not provide job or grant incentives for youth, such as those created in New York, the Miami organization is now part of a two-year, limited, and nonfinancial collaboration by several Ecuadorian social clubs in the city. This group meets regularly to discuss and share information and to coordinate event calendars. The board representatives agree that they should help to promote one another's events.

The significant changes in organizational goals and functions are a dynamic of epistemological importance to the study of social organizations in anthropology. Based on the number of existing publications, interest already exists in these types of immigrant associations in branches of ethnic studies, political science, and sociology. Works that stand out in this category of scholastic literature include an ethnography about Mexican migrants, *Undocumented Lives: The Untold Story of Mexican Migration* (2018) by ethnic studies scholar Ana Raquel Minian, which focuses on the function of several social clubs whose missions often intersect. A classic study by Linda Basch about immigrant organizations in 1987 identifies nine categories of activities performed by these types of civic associations, including, but not limited to, political activism, benevolent activities, sports, social welfare services, and educational training. Speaking from both an anthropological and sociological perspective, Babis, analyzing existing scholarship in "Understanding Diversity in the Phenomenon of Immigrant Organizations: A Comprehensive Framework" (2016), expresses concern that remains valid about the slow pace of research in this area. Sociologist Maria Abascal (2015, 317) describes the ethnically and geographically different sites of this research as "communities—among the most likely to seek citizenship along with those faced by episodes of exceptional hostility." The testimonies that follow provide evidence that the individuality of each organization and the related construction of double-conscious identities by club members are directly related to the impact of context-based racialization in the adopted nation and the homeland.

Chapter 1:

Contextualized Migration: Ecuador, Los Angeles, Miami, and New York City

The homeland forces that pushed Ecuadorians to migrate have instigated domestic change throughout the nation's history. Periodically during the 20th century, Ecuador's traditionally marginalized formed unified masses to resist social denegation and the tyranny of the state. The Indian voice emerged through history to demand the creation of a new rhetoric that would abandon self-deprecating and stereotypical references to the pitiful or "miserable" Indian. Also, in the beginning of this same century a contingent of the middle class joined forces with military officers to put an end to a corrupt liberal political regime. Widespread domestic unrest erupted that crossed lines of ethnic and class difference, resulting in the election and overthrow of a total of 15 political administrations during the 1930s. To make matters worse, this period was marked by internal and external chaos. Rampant domestic political corruption was accompanied by both a rapid decline in exports of the primary national crop, bananas, and the global collapse of most international markets due to the Great Depression.

During the 1930s and 1940s, nationwide unrest within the ranks of the subaltern increased, and the campesinos—a multiethnic class of poor workers—demanded public policy changes to the hegemonic structure of the state and its institutions. Historically disadvantaged Ecuadorian communities began to seek equal access to their rights as citizens and to state resources such as education. The root causes were the oppressive dominance and greed of the land-owning elites and the federal government's unequal use in poor communities of production tax revenues. In the late 1940s, when crop disease curtailed exportation of bananas from Central America, Ecuador became the global leader in banana production.

The issue of land or agrarian reform took on greater significance after the 1950s in the sociopolitical struggle of the Indian and Afroecuatoriano. But the state used the high level of illiteracy among Indigenous Ecuadorians to justify restricting from voting by law. Literacy testing also served as a nativist tool to limit Afro-American voter participation in the United States from 1890 to 1965. In Ecuador, anti-disenfranchisement efforts on the part of the Indigenous, inspired by the U.S. equal rights movement, increased to press for government improvements to education for rural Indigenous communities. A formidable backlash by the economic elite, supported by the government, successfully resisted the demand for agrarian reform until the 1960s and 1970s. The poor became separated from their land, and many campesinos joined a decade-long national emigration of laborers to Ecuador's cities, including Quito, Guayaquil, and Cuenca.

Surges of impoverished former landowners of all ethnicities flocked to these urban centers. There they found a paucity of opportunities to work and restricted housing in ghettos or barrios, on the outskirts of cities like Quito and Guayaquil. As Carlos de la Torre and Catherine Conaghan (2009, 348) note, by the 1960s the bottom fell out of the Ecuadorian political economy due to the inequitable political and economic practices of a series of populist leaders. In summary, the entire period of 1960–2010 in Ecuador was marked by social and political changes that drastically hindered its citizens' ability to construct a life based on the balanced objectives of achieving within Ecuador what Arjun Appadurai (2004) refers to as a "good life." Appadurai conceives of the good life as developed in a context of social interaction and as involving the formation of ethics and ideas "about health and happiness" (68). My study found evidence that when the ability to imagine possibilities is unevenly distributed in societies, this condition is accompanied by a lack of access to means necessary to construct a good life and by a rise in transnational immigration. The good life is a characteristic of acculturation I examine in this study because—unlike the American Dream—the desire to create a good life is attached to the moral fiber of a society. Contrary to the American Dream, the good life is a resilient set of principled wants and choices that operates independent of fluctuations in national economics and politics.

In 2006, the sucre, Ecuador's national currency, failed and had to be stabilized by aligning it with the U.S. dollar. To add insult to injury, a decrease in industrial development and a rise in regional and internal conflicts revived old hatreds and suspicions based on ethnic and regional differences. Public discord intensified each day as economic necessity forced dissimilar cultural groups and social classes to live closer together in a shrinking urban social space. All these factors, combined with the rise of a globalized international economy and reduction of state social entitlements, set the stage for the reshaping of the personal priorities that motivate immigration (Bertoli et al., 2011) or the adoption of a transnational worldview (Foner, 2001). Perhaps O. Hugo Benavides (2004, 22) best summed-up Ecuador's political and economic status at the dawn of the new millennium and since: "As the Ecuadorian case indicates, a fragmented nation-state is an economic and political asset in the international-development arena."

Defining the Migration Waves and Destinations

As shown above, the 20th-century transfer of transnational artifacts, resources, and memories for Ecuadorian immigrants was driven by sociopolitical and economic change. This book's focus is on the population of current adults who left Ecuador, who began to experience a double-consciousness identity even as children, from the 1960s through 2010.

We now briefly turn to qualitative data to draw a few basic conclusions about the socioeconomic and ethnic status of individuals who joined the waves of migration from Ecuador to various international destinations. According to the U.S. Department of Home-

Figure 3.

Region and country of last residence	1930 to 1939	1940 to 1949	1950 to 1959	1960 to 1969	1970 to 1979	1980 to 1989	1990 to 1999	2000 to 2009	2010	2011	2012	2013
South America	9,990	19,662	78,418	250,754	273,529	399,803	570,596	856,508	85,783	84,687	77,748	79,287
Argentina	1,397	3,108	16,346	49,384	30,303	23,442	30,065	47,955	4,312	4,335	4,218	4,227
Bolivia	77	893	2,759	6,205	5,635	9,798	18,111	21,921	2,211	2,113	1,920	2,005
Brazil	1,468	3,653	11,547	29,238	18,600	22,944	50,744	115,404	12,057	11,643	11,248	10,772
Chile	568	1,320	4,669	12,384	15,032	19,749	18,200	19,792	1,940	1,854	1,628	1,751
Colombia	1,278	3,454	15,567	68,371	71,265	105,494	137,985	236,570	21,861	22,130	20,272	20,611
Ecuador	320	2,207	8,574	34,107	47,464	48,015	81,358	107,977	11,463	11,068	9,284	10,553
Guyana	193	596	1,131	4,546	38,278	85,886	74,407	70,373	6,441	6,288	5,282	5,564
Paraguay	36	85	576	1,249	1,486	3,518	6,082	4,623	449	501	454	437
Peru	460	1,273	5,980	19,783	25,311	49,958	110,117	137,614	14,063	13,836	12,414	12,370
Suriname	33	130	299	612	714	1,357	2,285	2,363	202	167	216	170
Uruguay	153	754	1,026	4,089	8,416	7,235	6,062	9,827	1,286	1,521	1,348	1,314
Other South America	2,647	7	17	28	18	2	-	2	1	2	-	1
Totals	28,610	56,804	225,327	731,504	809,580	1,177,004	1,676,608	2,487,437	247,852	244,832	223,780	228,349

Extrapolation of data from U.S. Homeland Security (2016).

land Security's Office of Immigration Statistics (Figure 3 Migratory Waves), from 1960 to 1980 approximately 81,000 Ecuadorians received a "green card," or permanent residence status, in the United States. The holder of this coveted "green card" was either sponsored by an employer or qualified due to family ties in the United States. Obtaining a green card enables the bearer to apply to take the examination to become a naturalized citizen. Brad Jokisch and David Kyle (2008) claim that the majority of this migrant flow was from southern Ecuador to the United States, while the second wave of migrants, from 1990 to 2000, left for not just the United States but also Spain and Italy.

The migratory passage most traumatic for the subjects of this study included being exposed to perilous situations as they crossed the Mexican border into the United States. Like the caravans of Central Americans cast as a threat to U.S. security under the Trump administration, Ecuadorians fell victim to unscrupulous coyotes (smugglers) and litigators on both sides of the border. Most traveled alone. Informants I interviewed spoke of the crippling impact of loneliness and how this influenced their lack of English proficiency. For many years, and with the objective of citizenship, they founded transnational civic organizations as spaces in which they could simultaneously celebrate both their Ecuadorian and U.S. cultural heritages. This study adopts the viewpoint of sociology and Latinx scholars to argue that the role of these clubs is to engender social networking (Portes, 1998) and a type of communal solidarity (Galván & La Vereda, 2006). Informant testimonies support this conceptualization of solidarity and show that community participation provides access to valuable knowledge as well as fosters the agency migrants need to survive and prosper in racialized societies.

This multisited investigation documents the process of acculturation by employing a contextually sensitive approach. The methodology adopted to do this ethnographic study reflects the influence of the directive by George Marcus (1995) that ethnographic studies should "follow the people, the narratives, and the conflicts." Approaching the work from this perspective facilitates analyses such as the upcoming discourse about varying class-based hegemonic social models and their related and very distinct productions of racialization. Race comes to the forefront—as does class and gender in the following intersectional exploration of the social climates of Los Angeles, Miami, and New York City. Each section below contains a subject testimony focusing on personal acculturation experiences.

Employing a multisited approach distinguishes this study from the small body of extant scholarship. For example, Pribilsky's (2007) focus in his research is on the transnational experiences of male-only members of Ecuador's rural-to-urban migratory labor class. Mills's (2004) intersectional ethnography asks many of the same questions about identity that I address here, but the subjects are from only one Ecuadorian region and the conclusions drawn about the impact of place on their cultural practices are not confirmed across different social climates in the United States. My central argument is that we are a sum-total of "our past and present" experiences (Bhabha, 1994) and that understanding the ambivalence of the process of self-identification on public surveys requires giving meaning to and documenting the intersectionality—or multifarious junction—of class, race, and gender that defines how anthropological subjects see themselves during any single period of time, or different ones.

Los Angeles and environs

Known throughout the world as a city of opportunity, the City of Angels inspires the quest to find and live the American Dream. But in this home of the American ideal did Ecuadorian migrants encounter a welcoming space? Did immigrants from Ecuador who arrived between the late 1960s and the early years of the new millennium feel they were treated as friends? Were they shown hospitality in Los Angeles as new arrivals? Many subjects interviewed for this investigation addressed these issues in their testimonies about adapting to the social pressures of settling in L.A.

Several questions speak directly to the always-present demand to be malleable—the required willingness to change at the drop of a hat that for many defines life in L.A. How would Los Angeles frame and influence Ecuadorian immigrants' construction of their lives? Were relationships between ethnic groups possible? If these coalitions exist, in what ways could they benefit Ecuadorian migrants? Spatial entitlement, or the exercise of cultural plasticity, enabled Latin Americans and other ethnicities to form multiethnic coalitions. The outcome, according to Gaye Theresa Johnson (2013), was the taking and making of spaces to stem the tide of racial and ethnic oppression. Ecuadorian subjects confirmed this when they spoke of their efforts to reconstitute public facilities such as parks and city streets for fiestas and parades, and to become part of the union labor movement. Laying claim to these spaces was a tactic shared by L.A.'s marginalized ethnic groups to create cultural citizenship. Cultural citizenship is membership in a community that serves as an alternative to the racialized and political definition of citizenship in the United States.

Johnson (2013, xx) argues that relationships between Latin Americans and Afro-Americans in LA during the mid- and late 20th century resulted in the formation of collaborative projects to overturn racial and ethnic oppression. One theory to explain the symbiotic relationship is that many prominent Afro-Americans romanticized what they believed to be the Mexican state's resistance to overt racism in the United States. The witness testimonies in this book broaden Johnson's evidence by recounting experiences when Latin Americans and Afro-Americans constructed zones of spatial entitlement on the job and in their neighborhoods. According to the informants I interviewed, these were critical times in their lives when they worked side by side in unions to oppose unfair hiring practices and with civil rights activists to expose human rights violations. Industrial extension projects during the 20th century included the creation of a massive highway construction program to accommodate residential expansion and the scattering of ethnic and racial groups that followed the city's development into sprawling suburban centers. In order to sustain a sense of belonging, shared public spaces in L.A. became centers of cultural celebration.

Latin Americans continued to join with Afro-Americans to create aesthetic and pragmatic expressions of their unity in the struggle for social, political, and economic equality (ix–xiv).

The 1970s and 1980s recessions were accompanied by a rise in the arrival of Latin American immigrants into the metropolitan area. Accompanying this influx was an increase in the inner-city presence of the homeless, a sharp increase in unemployment, and a widening abyss between the rich and the poor. According to Ruth Wilson Gilmore (2007, 57), one of the contradictions that resulted in the creation of two social classes in California was "Anglos' fear of their demotion to minority status, coupled with capital's differential exploitation of labor market segments defined by race, gender, locality, sector, and citizenship." The racist social climate that grew out of this paranoia, and a subsequent rise in national and local political demands for law and order, produced an economic engine in the state that tasked itself with managing surpluses of financial capital, land, and labor. Meanwhile, in 1994, draconian federal and state immigration policies culminated in the passage of Proposition 187, which cut public benefits to the undocumented. As the new millennium approached, inner city gentrification and the passage of the federal Illegal Immigration Reform and Immigrant Responsibility Act in 1996 deepened disparities between citizens and non-citizens.

Monica: Gender and Language in L.A.

The interview with Monica revealed much about the multiethnic cultural climate and acculturation process Ecuadorian immigrant children experienced in L.A. during the 1970s and 1980s. Various members of Monica's immediate family crossed U.S. and Ecuadorian borders several times in search of better social and economic opportunities.

Monica was born in L.A. in 1965. When she was four, her native Ecuadorian parents sent Monica and two of her four siblings to Guayaquil to become familiar with Ecuadorian culture. In Ecuador, family life took priority over community, and after her return to the

United States at age eight, Monica's parents restricted their children's contact with other kids in the historically and mostly Afro-American neighborhood of Pico Union (Sonenshein, 2013) to visits in their home. "My Mom opened the door to the Black kids to play with us, eat with us at times—but, she moved out of that neighborhood saying she wanted to 'get away from them' because of their different ways" (Monica, 2015).

Although Monica was permitted to invite Black children from her neighborhood to her house, conflicts among ethnic groups increased to the point that the family relocated after a few years to South Gate. As Monica recalled, the move was justified by her parents as their only way to escape both Afro-Americans and a wave of culturally different immigrants arriving in the neighborhood. Between 1960 to 1980, the percentage of Whites in Pico Union declined by over 60%, Blacks only increased their numbers by 1%, and the Latin American migrant population—comprised mostly of Mexicans, Salvadorans, and Guatemalans—increased by over 24% (Zhou & Lee, 2013).

By the late 1970s, when Monica and her family moved, Pico Union was an overcrowded slum in which the units were repeatedly being subdivided by greedy landlords (Loukaitou-Sideris & Hutchinson, 2006). The purpose of the transition was to accommodate an influx of what Monica's mother labeled as *cholos*. The meaning of *cholo* even today transcends transnational borders. *Cholo* is a term Ecuadorians used in the 19th and 20th centuries to denote landless Indigenous migrants or lower-class people (Roitman, 2008). The landmark scholarship of sociologist William J. Wilson (1987) analyzes Afro-American neighborhood deterioration prompted by the outflow of the middle class. Wilson's logic provides another explanation for the choice of the word *cholo* by Monica's mother to describe three ethnic groups in Pico Union: Afro-Americans, Mexicans, and Central Americans. Wilson claims that the decline of inner-city neighborhoods reflects their abandonment by upwardly mobile members of the middle class. The outflow of revenues, norms, and values results in a social, economic, and moral deterioration of formerly vibrant communities (138). Monica's mother, as an individual pursuing the American Dream for her children, used the term *cholo* to imply that her new neighbors were a part of a lower and threatening class. *Cholos*, to Monica's mother, were members of the transnational working class who failed to pull themselves up by their bootstraps to achieve the American Dream. Monica claims to have turned her mother's logic on its head when she became a special education teacher focusing on the uplifting of members of society who are often without boots or bootstraps.

In South Gate, Monica and her siblings were enrolled in a private Catholic school where language became less of an issue than in Pico Union. But her brush with prejudice in Pico Union and the acceptance of her Latin American heritage in South Gate are pieces of a puzzle that explain why Monica—who says her ancestral lines support her self-identification in Ecuador and the United States as White (*blanca*)—ethnically identifies in the United States as Ecuadorian. One of Monica's most interesting comments came when I asked her opinion about the labels commonly used in the United States to describe people from Latin America: *Hispanic* and *Latino/a*. "*Hispanic* sounds weird, too close . . . too attached to Spain—it's like we're a spinoff from Spain. *Latino* is someone from South America who speaks from that Latin [language] base, which includes all of us" (Monica, 2016). Regarding ethnicity, Monica also expressed confusion about the ethnic categories she finds on all types of questionnaires in the United States. She laughed and said she always fills out the "Other" category because she is aware Ecuadorians are known to be of various combinations of mixed ancestry, and it is highly likely that she too has Afro blood in her family.

During the 1970s, when Monica struggled to learn English in Pico Union, she and her mostly Mexican Spanish-speaking classmates were repeatedly ridiculed and even harassed by condescending teachers who imposed an illegal mandate that only English be spoken in school. Monica's progress was painfully slow, and the teachers often used it to justify sitting Monica with the other native Spanish speakers in the back of the classroom. As Monica's proficiency in English improved, so did her self-esteem and insistence that her parents' home also adopt the class-based English-only standard.

Monica provided the following explanation as to why she requires that her son of mixed Chilean and Ecuadorian heritage maintain pride in his dual cultural ancestry; "My mother said, 'Don't lose your culture, you come from Ecuador, you come from us" (Monica 2016). This expression of "keeping yourself" is the retention of homeland traditions, viewpoints, and languages shared by all the subjects I interviewed for this study.

Another benefit when Monica changed schools was that her parents and the mothers and fathers of her fellow students began to form a network of Ecuadorian friendships across L.A. This informal association led to the formation in the late 1970s of several Ecuadorian social clubs. Although most L.A. suburban communities like Pico Union and South Gate had few Ecuadorian families, Monica was the first interview subject who called my attention to the fact that organizations like the one formed by parents at her Catholic school now exist in many large U.S. metropolitan areas.

Over the years, Monica struggled with the incongruities and conflicts between U.S. and Ecuadorian ideas about race that she feels drives some mixed-race Ecuadorian immigrants and their descendants to abandon or dilute anything to do with their African heritage. By "dilute," Monica explained that she meant that individuals of mixed blood often take on the cultural traits of others and cut off ties with their Afro families—or in some cases even go so far as deny their African ancestry. She told me about a mixed couple from Ecuador, an Afro-Ecuadorian male and his *blanca*-mestiza wife, who immigrated to the United States in the 1970s to avoid racial tensions and the condemnation by their families in Ecuador. After the sudden death of the father, their children chose to marry or have relationships with ethnically different partners, including Afro-Americans, Afro-Latinos, and Whites. As Monica pointed out, interracial marriages are very common in Ecuadorian families all over the United States; but the reaction in many cases shatters the traditional custom to foster family unity when the new couple limits contact with their Ecuadorian family unit.

Ecuadorian migrants I interviewed in Los Angeles discussed the impact of stress factors and social relationships that they believe influenced their construction of self in L.A. and the environs. The interviewees validate Johnson's (2013) and Gilmore's (2007) claims that it was difficult for Latin Americans to build and maintain familial and community belonging in the widely dispersed multinational neighborhoods of Latin Americans in L.A. Also, the testimonies confirm that it was extremely important for most of the L.A. interviewees to establish intraethnic relationships both in the workplace and in their resident neighborhoods. The subjects spoke of the impact of working and living very close to other ethnic groups and the personal outcomes of cross-ethnic relationships that stood in opposition to the loneliness or absence of a sense of belonging. In each interview, there was also a discussion of class and the importance of acquiring English fluency to assimilate or culturally be cleansed of the alleged impurities or stereotypes associated with being an Ecuadorian Latin American. The informants' testimony sheds light on what is still today a process of cultural erasure in L.A., a city in which the predominant demographical statistics used to define the social climate are influenced by the notions that language proficiency denotes citizenship and that all Latin Americans are members of only two racial-nationalistic groups: either the "Mexican, noncitizen, non-English-speaker" or, the "non-Mexican, citizen, English-speaker" classes.

From the late 1970s to the 1990s, economic advancement in L.A. required that migrants become fluent in English. Even in the new millennium, speaking Spanish in some public spaces or having a Spanish accent is viewed as being low-class. The testimonies also revealed that in L.A. the Anglo fear of the lower class noted by Gilmore (2007) has been adopted by some Ecuadorian immigrants who struggle to distance themselves from membership in the ordinary or inferior classes by erasing their Spanish accents and embracing what they believe to be more acceptable identities. The sociopolitical project to erase Spanish was not found to be an objective in Miami.

Miami

Miami is a vast metropolitan microcosm in which Latin American diversity is the norm. However, the reality for emigrant South Americans in Miami who cannot claim or emulate Cuban ancestry is that their ethnic and cultural differences can prevent them from achieving success. Nigel Rapport and Joanna Overing (2000, 355) speak to the objective of trying to fit the dominant racial, class, and gender pattern or the process of acculturation, "the translation and mutual influencing that can occur when there is a new and rather sudden meeting between different world-views." Ecuadorian immigrants have survived despite being metaphorically treated as children by various classes of Miami's political and economic elite.

This section begins by focusing on the history of Miami from the 1960s through 2014 to examine two factors: (1) the impact of changes in the racial and ethnic composition of Miami's ruling class and (2) the way these culturally different elite groups framed and shaped the general feelings, attitudes, beliefs, and opinions of Latin American migrants. This analysis builds on the argument that the mission of Miami's various oligarchies has always been the same—to reduce the agency of specific national groups—especially those who have recently arrived (Grenier & Stepick, 1992). The collection of Miami testimonies provides personal glimpses of this as a fluid racializing process involving temporal changes and space.

Miami Powerbrokers and the American Dream

According to historian Chanelle N. Rose (2015), various groups of White business developers and political tyrants exercised complete control over Miami from the city's incorporation in 1896 until the era of the civil rights movement in the 1960s. During this time, Miami was a typical southern metropolis in which White powerbrokers used racial stratification to prevent people of African descent from playing a role in the construction of the city's social climate (1–2). But sociologists Elizabeth Aranda, R. E. Chang, and Elena Sabogal (2016) claim that with the arrival of fleeing Cubans in the 1960s, a nativist strategy based on language differences (English versus Spanish, Cuban Spanish versus Central American Spanish, and Mexican versus Cuban Spanish) and Latin American cultural norms and values conflated the Black/White strategy in a way that continued Miami's racialization in favor of phenotypical and cultural Whiteness. The result was an ethnic class-based changing of the guard and the distribution of power that continues to shape intercultural relationships and domestic institutions in Miami (150–155).

Unlike in Los Angeles, where English proficiency is a highly valued social resource and use of Spanish is not uniformly considered an asset, Spanish is Miami's most utilized language. Recent scholarship by sociologist Monika Gosin (2019) focusing on Afro-Cubans in Miami supports the contemporary validity of the claim that immigrants with a high level of competency in reading, writing, and speaking Spanish and those with the ability to fluidly switch between English and Spanish (Aranda et al., 2016; Carter & Callesano, 2018) effectively use these skills in Miami as social capital to construct support networks and gain employment.

Regarding the fluidity of Miami's hegemonic social structure, Arnada et al. (2016) also claim that beginning in the 1980s elite Cubans and multiethnic entrepreneurs gradually assumed control of Miami's wealth and politics in response to increased immigration to the city by Central and South Americans and the exit of both Whites and Blacks. The result of these changes is that having or not having citizenship, acquisition or failure to achieve the American Dream, class, and race are the intersecting axes along which modern Miami's autocrats currently stratify the city (150–159). The structure of the U.S. racialized and White-centric social model is a dynamic global apartheid, "the biggest threat to human rights and to human life and life chances, particularly for racially subjugated peoples" (Harrison, 2002). Global apartheid is a context-specific force that shapes Ecuadorian migrant acculturation in Miami differently than in Los Angeles. Ecuadorian migrants in this study speak to how achieving the American Dream may or may not be related to the ways their Ecuadorian customs and values are retained and assimilated into Miami's complex multiethnic cultural landscape.

Ronald Gonzalez: Mixed-Race and Maleness in Miami

Born in 1979, Ronald attended public school for many years outside his racially and ethnically mixed neighborhood in East Little Havana. Riverside Park is in the center of this community that Ronald said was referred to as "Vietnam." Even though the space is designated by the city as a public recreational zone, for many years the park has actually served as a neutral territory maintained between Cuban and Central American gangs. Ronald is second-generation, defined as having one or more parents who were born outside the United States. His dark complexion and self-identification as a person of Ecuadorian/Cuban and Latin American heritage born in the United States shaped his experiences as a student in Miami's public schools. He states, "I hung out with the *mulatos*, creoles, mostly from the Caribbean, and some Cubans, the mixed kids, and the other group was Central American. Kids off the boat looked different—some Cubans came in the 1980s—their outlook was more mature, more experienced in life because they had been through some bad things. . . . Some were delinquent . . . a lot of bad apples. Many folks older, in their 30s, had been released from jail in Cuba. Central Americans were fleeing war, but gangs from Central America set up headquarters in Miami, and kids joined. Kids who had witnessed horrible stuff in Central American wars" (Ronald, 2016).

The stress and conflicts in "Vietnam" grew out of the area's cultural and racial diversity and the lack of positive adult leadership and examples. Ronald was the exception in his neighborhood, where single mothers were left alone to raise children who watched and eventually joined their fathers selling or taking drugs in Riverside Park. Even the public school system failed to provide a consistent and uplifting atmosphere for the children of "Vietnam."

The public elementary school close to Ronald's home in East Little Havana was under construction for many years. This resulted in Ronald and his peers being bused to public schools throughout the city. Ronald was sent to Douglas Elementary in Overtown, a then- and still-decaying, mostly Black section of Miami that had once been a flourishing tourist enclave. During this era (1980–

1990s) in Miami, Rubén Rumbaut and Alejandro Portes (2001, 98) claim, the assimilation of children—a necessary component to support their upward mobility—depended upon which school they attended; middle-class migrants' children sent them to private schools, while lower-class and often first-generation immigrant children attended public schools staffed by less-qualified teachers.

Ronald is grateful that his parents ignored the warnings widely circulated in the community to avoid what was referred to as the "lower-class" Overtown schools. At Douglas and later in middle school in the same district, Ronald was a member of the majority because of the dark color of his skin. White students, in contrast, frequently found themselves the victims of discrimination in Overtown: "There was the last day of the school year, 'beat up a cracker day'—when we had a White beat-down day—if your skin was too light you would be beat up. It was that simple" (Ronald, 2016). Black-White racism was turned on its head in Overtown. But when Ronald was reunited with the kids from his neighborhood at Booker T. Washington Middle School in Little Havana, he says that it became clear that three factors would shape the future of his multiracial and multicultural generation: (1) ideas about race, class, and gender that are part of the racialization process of Miami, (2) the absence in the majority of "Vietnam" families of male positive role models, and (3) a related increase in the responsibilities of often first-generation migrant women left alone to assimilate children in an unfamiliar environment where males were often deeply involved in often-illicit gang activities.

"There were problems that got worst [*sic*] in middle school—all of a sudden the issue of race was in your face. People started forming cliques. Black kids the majority, Cubans, everybody else . . . the teachers were constantly talking about race. They [other students] even beat up my little brother Ricky and constantly picked on him so bad that after he was in our school for only about two months, my mom and dad had to take him out." In a later conversation Ronald claimed that the bullying of Ricky was because his brother is very quiet and lighter in complexion. "Some [of the children] did adjust. Some did eventually get a great job, others that joined gangs didn't . . . no father in home or strong leadership to prevent them from joining a gang. . . . A good role model made the difference. Assimilation was the goal, some failed and many, too many, joined gangs. Once they got a record with the law in Miami, that was it . . . no way to escape or improve" (Ronald, 2016).

Oliver Jütersonke, Robert Muggah, and Dennis Rogers (2009) claim that the violence practiced by Latin American *maras* (transnational gangs) that function in both Central America and the United States—have their origins in hegemonic masculinity, or machismo. The twisted codes of *maras* legitimate aberrant acts that adversely affect the lives of their own families, such as the sale of drugs in their own communities and the creation of a gun-centric culture in which violence is the norm (378–379).

During the interview, Ronald was ambivalent about identifying with any of the racial and ethnic categories. As he explained his position, he discussed the meanings of these classifications in terms of his lived experiences in two intersecting worldviews: (1) the norms, and values of his Cuban and Ecuadorian parents, which included the strong influence of ideals such as living a "good life," and (2) Miami's racialized interpretation of the American Dream, which always relegated particular Latin Americans to the bottom of the social ladder. The lens Ronald used to see beyond Overtown and "Vietnam" also enabled him to come to the conclusion that "American is synonymous with success, and the American Dream is a class-based achievement made possible because in the U.S. money rules" (Ronald, 2016). Ronald's viewpoint was advanced by T. H. Marshall (1950, 84), who argued that U.S. citizenship does not imply "equality of income." Building on Marshall, Anna Jefferson (2015, 311) calls attention to the meritocracy associated with the class-based American Dream that personalizes both success and failure, while creating a social hierarchy in which "citizenship will always be at odds with capitalism."

Ronald concluded with his opinion that the city and county's repeated failure to fund or even promote the work of community leaders and positive role models such as his father in Overtown and "Vietnam" relates directly to the fact that many children in these neighborhoods were never able to develop dreams of succeeding in the United States. Because Ronald did have excellent leadership and examples in his home, his plan to construct a successful future included the construction and utilization of the social capital he found inside and outside the Little Havana community.

New York City Spatial Mobility and Cultural Diversity

A term often used to describe New York City is "multiethnic community." The vast city is comprised of five boroughs—Manhattan, the Bronx, Staten Island, Queens, and Brooklyn (Figure 4 NYC Boroughs)—and in each the population of U.S. and non-U.S. citizens is ethnically diverse. Activists and educators argue that the plasticity (as in L.A.) of neighborhoods and the inherent tensions between residents is a norm. The following is an examination of the impact of changes since the late 1960s in the ethnic, racial, and class

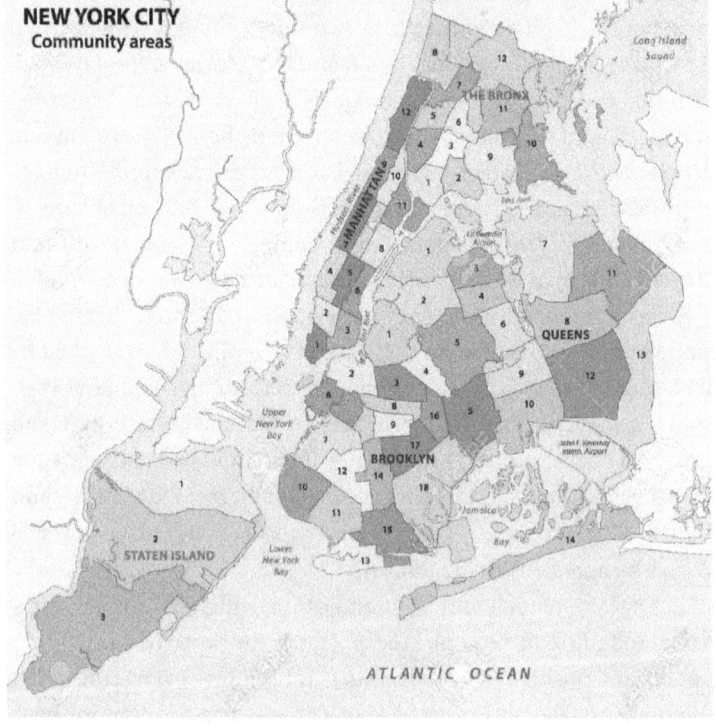

Figure 4. New York City's five boroughs.

hegemonic structure of communities such as Elmhurst-Corona in Queens and how shifts in the social climate of New York City influenced the lived experiences of migrants from Ecuador.

This section builds on the celebrated ethnographic study by Roger Sanjek examining the consequences of conflicts and collaborations between various immigrant populations in New York and how these intersected and shaped social, economic, and political circumstances inside and outside the Elmhurst-Corona community. In addition to Sanjek (2000), this research expands on Pribilsky's (2007) landmark investigation that examines the concept he refers to as Iony. Iony is the lens Pribilsky employs to study the consumption of specific products by undocumented Ecuadorian males in New York City and how these purchases impact the cultural context in the homeland (325). Existing anthropological scholarship specifically about Ecuadorian immigrants in New York City is a dated and narrow body of knowledge. For this reason, the approach in this part of the narrative—like the preceding sections on Los Angeles and Miami—is to incorporate post-2007 interdisciplinary scholarship with this project's empirical data and extant opinions about this population. For example, I will briefly discuss sociologist Sonia Song-Ha Lee's (2014) exploration of the hierarchy of specific Latin American nationalistic groups in New York City politics and Héctor Cordero-Guzmán's (2005) analysis of the role of community organizations in the city to elucidate Sanjek's (2000) historical study of New York's social and political environment. The first part of this section is a historical examination of late 20th- and early 21st-century prevailing feelings, beliefs, and opinions about the shifting social and political agency of Latin Americans in the city.

The Sociopolitical Structure of Elmhurst-Corona

According to Sanjek (2000), prior to the late 1960s, a White-majority population controlled the social and political climate of the two Queens neighborhoods of Elmhurst and Corona. But after the first influx of Latin American immigrants dominated a flow of various ethnic groups into the community, White exodus accelerated to the point that the New York City media and exploitative poli-

Figure 5. Queens Borough: Elmhurst, Corona, Jackson Heights, and Woodside communities.

ticians began to refer to Elmhurst, Corona, and Jackson Heights—in sometimes disparaging terms—as predominately Latin American enclaves. Ecuadorians who were part of several Latin American waves of immigrants to these three communities and Woodside (Figure 5 NYC Corona) between the late 1960s and early 1990s found storefronts closed and jobs scarce in the four neighborhoods except for a few in sweetshops that were a part of New York's declining apparel industry. By the 1990s, Latin American immigrants had become a part of the white-collar labor force that sustained the concept of "World City" coined by Mayor Edward Koch. The idea of World City envisioned New York as a global center of banking, business, and the fine arts. In practice, both Mayors Koch (1978–1989) and later David Dinkins (1990–1993) diverted federal funds earmarked to rejuvenate impoverished communities toward the construction of Manhattan infrastructure (64–142).

In the neighborhoods, Latin American immigrants negotiated the complex processes of assimilation and acculturation in communities in which ethnic origins, race, and class strongly divided the residents. The prevailing belief in New York was that new immigrants stole less desirable and menial factory and service industry jobs from citizens. This notion created a class binary in which native-born and naturalized citizens were pitted against "illegal aliens." Miles (2004, 186) sheds light on the implications of this xenophobia from the Ecuadorian immigrant perspective: she argues that Ecuadorian migrants understand both the process of racialization—based on class and ethnic differences—and the stratification of social and economic opportunities in the United States using the rubric of their lived experiences in Ecuador. But knowing why one is a victim of prejudice and discrimination does not lessen or change the realities that caused one's victimization.

Many New York City communities in the late 1990s became domains in which the residents suffered greatly because of the unequal distribution of social and economic opportunities and a rising level of ethnic chaos among neighbors. For example, reduced government subsidies for schools in the city reduced the quality of free-public education, forcing Latin American residents concerned about the quality of the preparation of their children for the future in Elmhurst-Corona to invest limited household funds in the parochial private school system. Also, by the late 1990s, the numbers of crimes involving violence against people of color escalated in the boroughs and included the 1994 chokehold death of Puerto Rican Anthony Baez (1994) at the hands of a White police officer and the hate-crime killing of Ecuadorian immigrant Manuel Aucaquizphi. Aucaquizphi's racist killers saw him as a "Mexican" trying to invade their space, a community park.

Misconceptions in the public domain about phenotypical differences and the value of Latin American immigrants during the late 20th century produced a mixed bag of interethnic relationships in New York City. One undeniable result was that racist notions of inferiority and superiority were used to deny equal housing and employment opportunities to the ethnically diverse and stratified residents of Elmhurst-Corona (Sanjek, 2000). Even within the arena of political advocacy, some national Latin American groups with greater numbers exercised more political agency than other national groups. One example is the Puerto Ricans, who often used their numerical strength to advocate for smaller Latin American groups (Lee, 2014; Cordero-Guzmán, 2005). Ecuadorians by 2008 were the fourth-largest Latin American population in the city (Caro-López, 2011); but, as with other South and Central Americans, many were not counted in official surveys because they were not citizens.

Elmhurst-Corona has many restaurants and social clubs that offer a variety of Latin American cuisines and cultural entertainment—sometimes under one roof. A report written by Howard Caro-López (2011, 3) and published by the City University of New York's Center for Latin American, Caribbean & Latino Studies (CLACLS) indicates that in 2010 Queens borough still had the highest concentration of immigrants from Ecuador because in neighborhoods like Elmhurst-Corona many well-established businesses cater to Latin American migrant populations. For example, the Ecuadorian-owned Delgado Travel Agency in Jackson Heights specializes in wiring money between the United States and Ecuador. Very basic counseling support, which does not include financial or job training, is provided in Woodside by a satellite office of the Ecuadorian consulate. Most U.S. Ecuadorians in the community are first-generation, and in 2008 the median household income of Ecuadorians was over $55,000 (11). But since 2005, Elvin Wyly, Kathe Newman, Alex Schafran, and Elizabeth Lee (2010) claim, aggressive gentrification had brought change. The result is that many ethnic groups, including Ecuadorians, are being forced out of Elmhurst-Corona (2612–2614). Concurrently, since 2008 two other trends involving migrants from Ecuador have been shaping the Queens borough: the arrival in the city of a large number of well-educated Ecuadorian immigrants and a significant rise in the number of Ecuadorian migrants entering the United States who do not have a high school diploma (2–15).

Leonor

In the homeland, an apprenticeship with a local seamstress taught Leonor critical life skills required to manage money and that rising from the lower class would be extremely difficult. Based on her experiences in Ecuador, Leonor, a featured subject throughout this work, believed that even a solid marriage would not protect her from the instability of everyday life as an Ecuadorian citizen. As Leonor approached the end of her apprenticeship with the seamstress, she searched for a way to fulfill two dreams: (1) to work in a profession that she had grown to love and (2) to support her mother after high school. After graduation, Leonor got her first job and over the next seven years earned enough money to attain her dream of economic and personal security.

In the 1970s, Leonor's brother was the first to immigrate to the United States. The achievements of her sibling in his new country of settlement inspired Leonor to begin to think about migration. As an experienced seamstress, she felt professionally prepared to follow her brother, but by this time she was married and expecting her first child. For this reason, in 1980 her husband first migrated to New York City, and months later, Leonor followed him, leaving their now two children with their maternal grandmother. Leonor quickly found her first job as part of the undocumented labor force in New York's garment district. She recalls this time in her life as profoundly sad because she witnessed countless raids by U.S. immigration authorities that resulted in the deportation of many of her fellow workers. In 1982, Leonor was deported. After a few months in Ecuador, she illegally reentered the United States, finding a job in New Jersey. New Jersey was by that time the global center of the garment industry, and Leonor knew she could become a member of the local union. In 1989 Leonor returned to Ecuador to bring her children to the United States. After three years, the union sponsored her application for a green card, and in 1993 Leonor and all of her family members became U.S. citizens.

Leonor entered the United States at a time when quotas instituted as part of the 1965 Immigration Act and rising public anti-immigrant sentiment incentivized a reduction in legal avenues to citizenship for migrants from western hemisphere nations. The end result was an upsurge of multiethnic immigrant workers in the informal sector and a rise in the numbers of undocumented migrants from throughout the world—especially those with homeland roots in Latin America (Golash-Boza, 2015). Leonor described her fellow workers as a multiracial and multiethnic social network. Anthropologist Jane Collins's (2009) ethnography about the global apparel industry in New Jersey notes that during the 1980s the unions' most active members were Afro-American females. When Leonor became involved in her union's activities, its primary struggle was protecting the workers' jobs in an industry quickly offshoring to increase profits. The lessons she had learned in Ecuador about the importance of self-improvement guided Leonor when massive job reductions were imposed to accommodate the global growth of the garment industry.

Leonor retains her Ecuadorian citizenship, and when she completes applications in her homeland that ask for her nationality, she describes herself as "Ecua-USA citizen." As an official dual citizen, her path to self-improvement included finishing every course in her field that was offered by the Fashion Institute of Technology (FIT), with the goal of becoming a fashion designer. Because of her interest in developing supplemental courses and the training of upcoming designers she also completed classes at Manhattan Community College. She is now co-grant supervisor of her own program funded by FIT in conjunction with the Garment Industry Development Corporation. Changes in U.S. immigration policies and the economics of the globalized garment industry repeatedly intersected to shape her life. The passage in 1986 of the Immigration Reform and Control Act (IRCA) granted amnesty to migrants who had arrived in the United States before 1982. Although her official date of entry was after 1982, a relaxed public opinion at that time about immigrants and pressure from the unions enabled her to directly benefit from participating in several employer-based and trade-specific training programs. The IRCA was a de jure attempt by the Reagan administration to reduce the number of undocumented migrants. Unfortunately, the IRCA also included provisions to punish employers of the undocumented, motivating the owners to intensify their search for a legal source of labor outside the United States.

Leonor used the social capital she gained from her family and professional networks to fight an enemy she had first confronted

Figure 6. Leonor, event director 2016.

in Ecuador: class discrimination. According to Leonor, in the first years of her acculturation in the United States she battled to free herself from membership in the noncitizen class. Leonor's final comments (Figure 6 NYC Leonor Parade) are taken from a phone conversation in which we talked about her involvement in the Ecuadorian Civic Committee Nueva York (ECCNY) as a board member and event coordinator. Leonor worked for the New Jersey factory that sponsored her green card for 13 years. During the bulk of her employment, she was also a board member of the local union. Part of her responsibilities was scheduling cultural events that would support the board's plan to encourage cooperation among the factory's ethnically diverse workforce. A student recommended that she invite a speaker from ECCNY to present for a cultural event. The ECCNY representative suggested during his visit that Leonor allow her then-16-year-old daughter to compete in the foundation's Queen of the Carnival Pageant. Leonor agreed, thus beginning a more than 20-year relationship with ECCNY, which, as a board member, included supervising the educational programs and the annual pageant in which her daughter had been a contestant.

The New York City interviews reinforced the idea that the "good life" is a diachronic phenomenon whose characteristics reflect the interplay of good and bad political and economic circumstances and ideas about cultural differences in both the homeland and settlement country. The subjects' testimonies about their lived experiences show that these periodic shifts are brought about by oscillations in national policies, cultural ideologies, and ideas related to variations in human characteristics. As we have seen, various factors, such as the impact of liberal or draconian immigration laws, the concepts of machismo, and the American Dream shape social settlement outcomes for migrant populations in both different and similar ways across the three metropolitan social climates. For this reason, a logical next step is to question how these adopted individual priorities and aspirations intersect with homeland norms and values within the context of social organizations.

Chapter 2:

Social Networks: Los Angeles's Club Ancón and Robert's Altruistic Independent Organization

Club Ancón

Acculturation thrives within reconstituted spaces such as the social clubs established in major cities throughout the United States by Ecuadorian immigrants. In the context of this research, acculturation refers to a synergistic process involving homeland and settlement cultures which produces multifaceted outcomes that "may or may not involve increasing orientation toward majority-group culture" (Fox, Thayer, & Wadhwa, 2017, 406). The clubs' names provide evidence of each association's potential to produce varying types of social networks and cultural citizenship. In 2016, a published list of Ecuadorian social organizations in Los Angeles consisted of approximately nine clubs. Association names for the most part reflected the membership's province or city or origin. Several of the 18 civic groups had a mission-specific name, such as the Club Deportivo Amazonas (Amazon Sports Club), the Comité Cívico Ecuatoriano de California (Ecuadorian Civic Committee of California), and the Asociación Ecuatorianos Residentes en el Exterior (Association of Ecuadorians Residing Abroad). Only a few of regularly held meetings, and others appeared to no longer be in operation. The analysis of two of these organizations that follows examines two related questions: What issues associated with acculturation may be affecting these groups? And how might these issues be interacting to cause membership instability?

Classic anthropological theories about social organizations

argue that groups are nonstatic (Sahlins, 2013) and affected by both inside and outside forces that frame and shape even small organizations into communities (Douglas, 1986). My research found one contributing factor to the shared instability of Ecuadorian migrant clubs to be norms and values from the homeland, such as *mestizaje* and regional mistrust. Settlement adaptation in the quest to achieve the American Dream also influenced this complex issue. By focusing on the club social dynamics and informant stories about their particular Los Angeles experiences of acculturation, this study's attention remains on "keeping yourself"—forming a positive selfhood—as one of the most important outcomes of place-keeping.

Club Ancón occupies the middle suite of a one-story office building in the El Camino Village neighborhood of Gardena, approximately eight miles from downtown Los Angeles. The location is between two major highways, and many of the founding members still live within a 20-minute drive. The club is named after an oil-rich parish, now a tourist mecca, on Ecuador's coast, about 90 miles from Guayaquil. At the time of the onsite observation there were 15 members. Socioeconomic forces that shaped Los Angeles into a city of satellite economies also created a push mechanism that separated the descendants following job opportunities to abandon their old neighborhoods and as a result Club Ancón. In 1972, when the club was established by three coastal migrant Ecuadorians, the site was on Imperial Highway close to downtown L.A. The founders' mission was to provide a nurturing space that would enable Ecuadorians to unite and work on community projects in the United States and in Ecuador. A good percentage of the funds raised from celebratory events at the current Gardena location is still used to subsidize these altruistic projects. The small interior of Club Ancón is converted into a nightclub to host these cultural enrichment events. The club extends a special welcome to other Ecuadorian social organizations and Latin American celebrities and guests. A major focus of the organization's governing body is participation in an annual parade in downtown L.A.

Each year the members select by vote a young woman of Ecuadorian heritage whom they sponsor to compete to be the reigning queen of the Fiestas Patrias Ecuatorianas (Celebration of the Ecua-

*Figure 7. Judy Olvera,
"La Morena k Canta,"
Valentine's at Club Ancón.*

dorian Homeland), a weeklong parade and food festival held in downtown L.A. The parade serves as an act of solidarity for Ecuadorian migrants who may or may not be members of one of L.A.'s nearly 15 Ecuadorian clubs. It is not uncommon for other Latin American groups to sponsor floats or send representatives to the event. Ecuadorian independence from Spain serves as a central theme. In this way, the unified action of Ecuadorians produces the sociopolitical agency that results in a "transformation of a space into a place" (Low, 2009) of significant cultural meaning. Below is a brief description of one of the nightclub-like events I attended in 2015.

When I arrived at Club Ancón, the club's décor reflected the theme of the evening—Valentine's Day. A counter within one of the small rooms served as a bar. There were pictures on the wall of former Club Ancón officers. To the right of the kitchen was another oblong room with tables surrounded by chairs and arranged to free up the middle of the floor for dancing.

For the first hour, the crowd was light. The second hour the beer and mixed drinks began to flow, and the DJ's selection of music gradually changed until he settled into a mix of U.S. and Latin American music. By then, the crowd had almost tripled, and the small archway in front of the kitchen became the event epicenter. The remainder of the evening this small cozy area was where people hugged each other as they balanced plates of *seco de chivo* (goat), sweet cheese-filled empanadas, and beverages.

The room was absolutely packed after the arrival of Judy Olvera, "La Morena k Canta" (Figure 7 LA Judy Singer), the entertainer for the evening. Born in Guayaquil, she self-identifies as an Afro-Ecuadorian and now lives as a Latin American or Latina in Manhattan. She is part of what she described as a loosely connected group of musicians from various South American countries who travel throughout the United States entertaining at Latin American social clubs and special events. I would meet other members of this quasi-organization in Miami and New York City. They could be described best as the founders of new paradigms, creating spaces that foster cultural citizenship inside as well as outside traditional Ecuadorian social clubs.

Patricio: Club Ancón's President

The interviews explored so far revealed that there was no real tangible Ecuadorian settlement in Los Angeles from the 1960s to the 1990s. Instead, settlers from Ecuador followed employment opportunities or abandoned violence-prone neighborhoods in the inner city to establish new homefronts in one of L.A.'s multiethnic outlying cities. This meant that for many years they needed to rely heavily on familiar ties or the friendship of strangers who might not even speak Spanish. Also, subjects testified that for one reason or another they repeatedly moved throughout the city. Therefore, for long periods, they were without the social and economic benefits that come from being a part of a neighborhood in which the majority of the residents share cultural values and even some life experiences.

Patricio, chief executive officer of his own tax firm with offices in Lawndale, felt his six years of university education in the homeland would work to his advantage in L.A. At the time he began contemplating a move to the United States, Patricio hadn't finished his law degree. But he felt confident that he could earn enough money to either complete the degree abroad or finish it in Ecuador. He was also sure that he could build a new life by starting with the connections he thought that his sister had already made over the years after migrating to L.A. These hopes were dashed when his family received a letter from his sister in which she confessed to being overwhelmed by feelings of loneliness. She spoke of a sense of detachment and yearning to just speak her language with another Ecuadorian the way she did at home. According to Patricio, "The U.S. reputation was one of danger, you must avoid contact in U.S. society to stay safe. Also, Ecuadorians do not trust other Ecuadorians, and this stems from ideas in Ecuador that still prevail, like geography still matters—where in Ecuador you were born" (Patricio, 2016).

One similarity between Patricio and Robert—the second club president featured in this section—is that both were born in Ecuador's high sierra. Although Patricio is dark-complexioned, he does not appear to be Indigenous because his hair is not straight but wavy, and he has mostly White features. In Patricio's case, his life experiences began in Cotopaxi, south of Quito. Based on his Spanish ancestry on both sides, he describes himself as *blanco* (White) in both Ecuador and the United States, "despite my dark complexion, which makes me different than my whole family. I'm *blanco* . . . Hispano here in the United States. My mom is White-looking with green eyes, and so is my dad. I'm the only dark one in the family. But everyone loved me, I was treated special" (Patricio, 2016). Patricio feels he has never experienced discrimination in the United States based on racial difference. His opinion is that class and gender differences in U.S. society result in as much stratification as misconceived notions about race. When I asked him what he thought was the outcome of so much class conflict in the United States, he replied, "In the U.S. you are valued for what you have, people then think they are important. In Ecuador we socialize more, we live more, we share with people. In the U.S. you do everything for yourself. Not many people in the U.S. work with the community" (Patricio, 2016).

Above, Patricio is speaking about the absence in the United States of the communal ideal of the good life. He clarified this observation by saying that this feeling of being a part of the community is what inspired his mother to do charity work with the poor in the Ecuador. Patricio's mother was an employee of Ecuadorian Social Security. She encouraged her children to go outside their middle-class comfort zones to serve in some way the less fortunate. Patricio takes pride in his father's work ethic, and like the patriarch of his family he does not tolerate mistreatment of his family or employees for any reason. Patricio feels that hegemonic masculinity or machismo in Ecuador did not have much impact on his life. According to him, his father was always present and remained positive even after a bad investment caused him to lose his farm.

Patricio left Quito for the United States out of concern for his sister in 1979. From the standpoint of U.S. immigration policy, this was an optimal time to enter the transnational migratory channel. A movement was underway under the Immigration and Nationality Act (aka Hart-Cellar Act) to abolish national quotas and stimulate an increase in the number of permanent residents. This first trip was on a visitor visa because Patricio thought he could earn enough money to finish a law degree in Quito in just one year in the United States. This year passed quickly, and by 1982 Patricio had a thriving business selling goods by going from swap meet to swap meet in L.A. His connection to his settlement nation became even stronger when that same year and prior to Ronald Reagan's signing of the 1986 Immigration Reform Act (which granted amnesty to about 3 million undocumented immigrants) he became a U.S. citizen. His marriage in the late 1980s to a *mexicana* only increased his economic and family ties to the United States.

When I asked if he ever wanted to return to Ecuador, Patricio's voice softened as he confessed that even after the birth of his two children he always wanted to go back home. For him, this was the space in which he wanted to continue building his original dream: to be an attorney—a professional—and serve the young people of the community. For this reason, Patricio and his sister invested a substantial amount of money in the late 1980s to build four units in their homeland. Every penny of these funds was lost due to financial instability in Ecuador. Patricio said he had to file for bankruptcy. To save money, he sent his wife and kids to Ecuador, where the children stayed and attended school for three years while he began a 10-year process to repay debtors. In 2004, after the bills were settled, Patricio and his sister received invitations to attend an event at Club Ancón.

During his first visit to Club Ancón, Patricio enjoyed the music and food. After two years of attending club events, the members invited him to be president. Patricio was aware at that time that Club Ancón was traditionally controlled by his countrymen and countrywomen from the coastal zone. Despite the rumblings in opposition to his appointment, Patricio has always performed his duties in a way he feels ignores Ecuadorian stereotypes tied to geographical spaces. The method he uses to overcome these homeland notions is to provide a family-safe environment for all Ecuadorian immigrants. He emphasized how important this is to Ecuadorians who may attend the club's events while feeling threatened by the possibility of deportation. "It costs over $10,000 for some to cross the border. . . . It's dangerous, some have to pay coyotes. . . . So, when they arrive, they look for a safe place. Some Ecuadorian immigrants don't succeed here. Why? First of all because they love Ecuador; nobody comes with the idea to stay here. They say, 'I go to the U.S. to make money and then return,' they go back whenever possible. . . . But here, Ecuadorians work two or three jobs, they work hard and it takes a lot of money to be here. You must have an education to get a visa in Ecuador and have some type of work in the U.S. before coming. Even though it would be possible for other Ecuadorians to sometimes help them, generally nobody does this. . . . Ecuadorians don't trust other Ecuadorians; the old ideas prevail. . . . That's why there are many clubs in L.A. because geography [sierra vs. coast] still matters" (Patricio, 2016).

When Patricio gave the testimony above, he called attention to the traditional problems faced by Club Ancón, but he ended this statement about the current state of the organization by adding that there were new issues, like the fact that many members now live more than 30 to 50 miles from downtown L.A. As our conversation concluded, Patricio sat back in his chair. After thinking for a moment, he spoke briefly about a new dream that is also a commitment: he hopes to find ways to overcome the distance and to serve a younger and more Americanized generation at the club.

The success Patricio has attained as an entrepreneur is an indication that he feels he has achieved the American Dream. Through the transnational missions of the clubs in Ecuador, this also means that Patricio is now living the ideal good life of his past imagination in the homeland. When I asked which of the two life ideals he hopes to promote at the club, Patricio stressed that he has constructed a new identity that reflects the values of a good life in a domain dominated by the ideal of the American Dream. Patricio's place-making reflects his desire to maintain or keep a positive selfhood, keeping yourself while serving others.

Robert: Dreams, Success, and Altruism

The eruption of Ecuador's Cotopaxi that lasted from August 2015 to January 2016 prompted Club Ancón and other U.S. Ecuadorian organizations to develop quick solutions to deliver aid to the homeland. The first subject I met at a fundraiser in Pasadena dedicated to this purpose was the priest (*pastor*) Joselo. El Pastor brought to my attention the existence of many small clubs or groups of Ecuadorians who have formed nonprofit organizations based on commonly held personal beliefs. These groups create spaces of solidarity and mobilization to support Latin Americans directly threatened by the political forces of global apartheid. He mentioned the work of his brother Robert, whom he strongly encouraged me to visit. He described his sibling's organization near Riverside as a religiously inspired project with service commitments in undocumented Latin American communities throughout the United States and in rural and historically neglected provinces in Ecuador.

The interview with Robert took place in his office in the arid Fontana foothills, about 50 miles from downtown Los Angeles. He admitted to feeling a bit overwhelmed by events surrounding an unexpected natural catastrophe and a need to prepare to personally deliver emergency aid in Ecuador. This interview occurred shortly after April 16, 2016, when an earthquake measuring 7.8 on the Richter scale caused a tremendous amount of property damage, injury to over 28,000 people, and more than 650 deaths in the province of Esmeraldas. Robert's small office near the front of the building was full of articles to be placed in the shipping container that sat in the hallway. He took phone calls during the interview about the logistics of delivering the relief. Some of the calls were about his plans to travel to Ecuador to personally bring spiritual and tangible support to what he later described as the most impoverished regions of his homeland.

During the two-hour interview, Robert spoke of the importance of having a strong work ethic and how owning All One Auto Center and Dismantling (Figure 8 LA Robert Business) represents his success and the freedom to live the American Dream: "To me it means preparation, get a house. . . . Everyone wants a house, boys want a first car, then a house, then you meet someone special . . . marry and form a good family, have property for kids to live in, working and having some money" (Robert, 2016).

Figure 8. Aid earmarked for Ecuador outside the entrance to Robert's office.

Robert, who was born in Chimborazo in the high sierra near Cuenca, has dual citizenship and identifies as mestizo (Spanish and Indigenous) in Ecuador. Because he feels there is no such category to describe him on the U.S. census, he self-identifies in the United States as ethnically Ecuadorian and racially "Other." A self-described pragmatist, Robert expressed disappointment that being an "Other" means that in many ways in the United States he does not exist.

Invisibility is not an unfamiliar problem for Robert. He recalls being the victim of discrimination in Ecuador because of his dark features and small frame; in college, other students taunted him because of his poor background and the way he spoke Spanish. Robert's homelife tended to be unstable due to his father's drinking. His father was not a philanderer. In fact, and in many ways, he practiced charity and genuine caring for the culture and well-being of the Indigenous people in the region surrounding Quito. Unfortunately, his father would often disappear for long periods, until his wife and children found him drunk in the streets of Quito. According to Robert, although his father could not control his drinking, when he worked as a construction foreman, he was highly respected.

Robert's memories of his father reveal the sources of his belief that living a good life requires a strong work ethic, a dedication to preparedness, and the willingness to train the next generation to care about the suffering of others. Despite being an alcoholic, his father was not the stereotypical adulterer, with multiple unclaimed children, and he did not physically abuse his wife and children. But he only worked sporadically, often forcing Robert to assume the role of breadwinner for the family. Robert has learned over the years to value his ability to overlook differences in race, class, and ethnicity—something he said he learned from his father. This would prove to be a valuable skill as Robert worked side by side in the fields and factories with people of different races and classes in Ecuador and the United States.

At age 20, Robert graduated from high school. Later he announced to his family, "I'm going to the U.S., the land of opportunity—land of Martin Luther King, where everything is possible. . . . You'll have an opportunity if you work and respect the laws. In the U.S. it doesn't matter if they discriminate against me, my mind is ready to go over there—where I can save money. Money to me meant security" (Robert, 2016). Clearly, Robert was aware that his physical appearance, as well as class and racial differences in Ecuador, could create problems again for him in the United States. However, these concerns were tempered by his hope that his experiences in Ecuador as a hard worker and his ability to navigate class and racial discrimination all would work to his advantage once he migrated to the United States.

In 1988, Robert arrived in Los Angeles with a high school diploma and one year of college. He doubled his clothes each day to cover his skinny frame, at only 117 pounds, and took a job in downtown L.A. in a warehouse. On and off this job, the ability to ignore racial difference that he learned from his father was reinforced by strangers from different ethnic groups in the United States. As Robert struggled one day at his factory job to lift boxes that weighed almost as much as him, several Afro-American workers used gestures to communicate to Robert that they wanted to help him. To make sure Robert was able to keep his job, his fellow employees permanently reorganized the work in a way that would require Robert to only lift weight that was appropriate for his body size. The actions of his coworkers echo more public attempts to unite Latinos and Afro-Americans, such as a promise in the late 1960s by Latino activist and educator George I. Sánchez and Afro-American jurist Thurgood Marshall to collaborate on civil and human rights issues. Although neither the Sánchez-Marshall alliance nor an attempted joining of forces in 2002 by the League of United Latin American Citizens and the National Association for the Advancement of Colored People resulted in any known public policy or institutional changes to overcome structural racism, Robert eventually met many Mexican, Asian, and Central Americans over the next 15 years who became part of his reliable social capital network of supporters and advisers.

Yolanda. Musical Identity and Activist Inspirations

The importance of a multiethnic network to the acculturation process of Ecuadorians in Los Angeles emerged as an issue in all L.A. testimonies. For example, Yolanda, a 70-year-old renowned singer who migrated from the Andean province of Imbabura near Colombia, described many instances when non-Ecuadorians shaped her social destiny in Los Angeles. After her 14th birthday, at her mother's insistence, Yolanda was sent to live with her sister in Quito to have better access to an education. She self-identifies in Ecuador as mestiza based on her mixed Spanish and Indigenous heritage. At age 10, she began singing in public by entertaining the crowds at voter registration rallies she attended with her mother. Yolanda told me that singing professionally had always been her dream. But to meet the demands of migration she considered it more practical to complete a course to become a paralegal and a secretary. This vocational training included a class in business English. Yolanda finally entered the United States with a green card by way of Tijuana after being denied a visa by U.S. embassies in Colombia, Panama, and Costa Rica. Over a two-year period and with each step toward the United States, Yolanda continued to sing to earn money, all the while keeping what she was sure was her greatest asset, her training as a paralegal, "tucked under my arm, protected—this I saved for the U.S." (Yolanda, 2016).

Yolanda used her family network and after her arrival at the home of her sister in L.A. immediately found work. Although the first job proved to too strenuous, her multiethnic coworkers, mostly Latin and Afro-Americans, were dazzled by Yolanda's renditions of Latin American songs and offered to take on her responsibilities. According to Yolanda, this support group did her job so well that she was promoted to oversee them as a manager. But she quickly resigned when she found out she'd have to inform on them as part of her new responsibilities. Yolanda got another break almost immediately and because of the encouragement of an Afro-American fellow employee went to evening classes to improve her everyday English. Existing literature exploring Afro-American linguistics provides evidence that Yolanda was engaged in the same class struggle in the United States faced by all those who do not speak Standard English (Spears & Hinton, 2010). Yolanda's Afro-American colleagues had good reason to identify with her desire to learn to speak, read, and write Standard English. Again, her network connections led to a very good job at Union Bank, with the opportunity to advance as she increased her English proficiency. All the while as she focused on her clerical talents to achieve the American Dream, she pushed herself further and further away from singing.

When asked to describe her relationships with other Ecuadorians in L.A. during the 1970s through the first decade of the new millennium, she answered, "I didn't find any Ecuadorians. I finally found one lady, a friend of my sister in Glendale. But I didn't find any others. My sister lived in Hollywood; she didn't have any Ecuadorian friends there either. I did start seeing more Ecuadorians around 1974. . . . In 1977, I met more Ecuadorian citizens when I became a U.S. citizen, got to know them at their restaurants. . . . I got a real estate license, in 1978 I started in real estate, but most of my customers were other Latin Americans and Black people. I first found out about the clubs in 2006 or 2007 for Ecuadorian people. . . . That's when I came back to the music, that's when I met Ecuadorian activist Elba Berruz. When I came back to the music" (Yolanda, 2016). Yolanda's eyes filled with tears as she spoke of her friend. According to Yolanda, Berruz's legacy is that she was a Latin American human rights activist who also cofounded many existing U.S. Ecuadorian social clubs. After her 1966 arrival in the United States, Berruz became a community organizer and coordinator. In 1994, she led the way to establish dual citizenship—the ultimate expression of bilateral and transnational belonging for U.S. Ecuadorian immigrants.

In her personal life, Yolanda also crossed geographical borders by marrying twice, first to a Bolivian, then, after this husband's sudden death, to a Guatemalan. Yolanda has performed in many Ecuadorian social clubs, but she avoids joining these organizations because she feels they "only support their own members and they just don't want to pay artists." For these reasons, and like Robert, she established her own nonprofit association to be able to provide an environment for all Latin Americans to come together to freely celebrate the rich artistic diversity of their homelands.

Robert also married outside the Ecuadorian community, to a Guatemalan immigrant in 1998. In the early years of the new millennium he enrolled at Freeman Occupational Center (FOC) in L.A. to train to be a computer technician. But without proper immigration paperwork and with only the technical English that was part of the FOC curriculum, he cleaned buildings until 2006, when he found a new job at a Korean body shop at the corner of Crenshaw and Olympia Avenues in midtown L.A. At his new job, Robert again followed his father's advice to always work hard. His manager—an Afro-American man Robert described as mixed-blood or *mulato*—noticed his dedication and, along with the Korean owners of the shop, supported his efforts to learn English and acquire the skill sets he still uses today to repair cars and care for customers. As Robert's children grew old enough to start their own lives outside the home, his wife also turned her attention to building a career. Robert encouraged her to go to college, and after completing a two-year degree she began working at a large savings and loan corporation.

During the early years of his settlement, Robert and his wife saved money. As Robert recalled, because he was a conscientious and industrious worker, he was eventually able to benefit from the support of his always-growing multiethnic network of friends, associates, and, in some cases, financial backers. Robert bought his mother a home and supported the efforts of his younger siblings—including El Pastor—to earn college degrees and enter the United States. Several years ago, Robert managed to even bring to the United States a nephew who will soon receive his college degree. As he invested money in his family in the United States and Ecuador, he also began to purchase real estate, buying four units in Van Nuys: "We saved because I wanted my own house—I saw renting just cost too much—not as a status symbol" (Robert, 2016). At the core, Robert's family home confirmed that he had acquired a space for his family to enjoy a balanced life by appropriating the ideal of the American Dream.

In 2008 as the chaos of a globalized modern world intensified with the crash of the U.S. economy, Robert made a fatal decision to increase his investment in the American Dream by opening his own business. His inability to meet financial obligations caused friction in the family, which eventually disintegrated as Robert and his wife invested more time independently preparing themselves to compete in a rapidly shrinking economy. The testimonies of this study's informants suggest that economic crises during migration and acculturation often cause irreparable damage to the family structure, calling into question the universality of Pribilsky's (2007) general claim that migration increases the value and meanings of family. The experiences of this study's subjects support the premise that, while it is possible to describe potential positive and negative outcomes of migration, it is impossible to assume any consistent impact of the migratory process on the family's local or transnational structure.

Circumstances went from bad to worse in the latter part of 2008. As Robert fought in the courts to evict a former tenant and struggled with little success to attract customers to his business during a recession, he resigned himself to divorce and to leaving the Van Nuys property of his dreams. For the next few years, Robert slept on the floor in what was then a shell of the commercial building that now serves as the offices of All One Auto Center. Robert has a long history of battling and winning against the formidable forces of various local and national U.S. legal institutions. Although he purchased All One Auto Center in 2003, the local authorities didn't grant approval to use the property until 2007. The complex legal conflicts over property and the social disappointments he faced as a divorced father were both challenges that threatened the dreams that Robert constructed in Ecuador and that he believed would come true in the United States.

As Robert continued to talk about challenging times in his life, he contextualized the story by reflecting on the lessons taught to him in Ecuador by his father and showed how these now influence his ideas about how to survive as an migrant in the United States: "I started helping other people, just like my father. . . . In 2007 I did a big case, one lady . . . an Indigenous lady, came here and she needed a flight ticket to get to her husband in New York City. . . . I helped her. A year later I received a call about a girl from Ecuador that was caught [by immigration] in Phoenix. . . . They asked me to adopt her. . . . I found out who to talk to get help and they agreed to help her. I was investigated to adopt her. But in 2007 they released her and they sent her back to Ecuador. I tried to get help in Ecuador with a nonprofit to bring her back to U.S. American institutions, and the U.S. government finally helped me. I brought her back here. She now stays with me. . . . A month ago she became a U.S. citizen" (Robert, 2016).

There are many examples of scholarship focusing on the social benefits of citizenship for White Cubans (Portes & Bach, 1985; Gosin, 2019). These studies often intersect with a rich body of literature examining the meritocratic and capitalist assumption that failure or success in achieving the American Dream is an individual responsibility (McNamee & Miller, 2009). There is space in this body of work for an intersectional analysis of the successful lived experiences of college-educated and non-White Latino immigrants like Robert. T. H. Marshall (1950) argued that the American Dream does not entitle any American to an income. Also, negative ideas rooted in both Ecuador and the United States about Robert's dark skin increase the likelihood that he will not enjoy the other benefit of this ideal as a citizen, an "equality of status" (85). But in Robert's case the opposite is true. His struggle during his settlement in the United States with anti-immigrant practices, and discrimination based on class and race, produced a similar outcome than the one I observed in the social clubs. When Robert refers to himself as a self-made millionaire and expresses his pride in obtaining U.S. citizenship for himself and most of his family, he is exercising free agency by claiming both the social and political rights associated with citizenship.

During his interview, Robert frequently mentioned that his determination to be an obedient servant of the Catholic Church has sustained him and makes him feel compelled to perform unselfish acts of kindness in the United States and Ecuador. In the sociological study *From Vietnam, Laos, and Cambodia: A Refugee Experience in the United States*, which features Vietnamese subjects, Jeremy

Hein (1995) adds clarity to Robert's claim, confirming that transnational political activism and altruism emerge within devout Catholic immigrant communities (Reed-Danahay & Brettell et al., 2008). Pribilsky's (2007) focus on Ecuadorian working-class migrants brings to light religious exercises of the imagination to create protective spheres or transnational landscapes of safety. In contrast, most of this study's Ecuadorians who claimed to have had high levels of preparedness or educational and vocational achievement prior to migration, did not mention the impact of religion in their lives. Pribilsky (2007) refers to such subjects who claim success as the elite or more settled immigrant class.

Although many questions related to the role of religion in the acculturation process are not addressed by this study, the fact that the Ecuadorian social clubs do not emphasize religious practices provides at least one possible reason Robert, who describes himself as a devout Catholic, prefers to create his own organization. Robert is no longer restrained by the norms of the social club network. He feels free to engage in political activism and philanthropic acts throughout the United States and Ecuador. Two factors explored in this research conjoin with Robert's Christian belief system to enable him to adopt a positive migratory identity and perform charitable acts: (1) his formation of a strong multiethnic, multiracial, and multicultural network of associates and friends to support his efforts, and (2) the impact of homeland and settlement beliefs, values, and practices in his construction of a successful U.S. identity.

Chapter 3

Professional and Personal Mobility: Miami's Liga Ecuatoriana de Florida and Vecinos en Acción

The concept of cultural citizenship has much in common with the Du Boisian double-consciousness theory. Chapter 2 brought to the surface the polar opposite and double-conscious outcomes of cultural citizenship: a sense of strong community and a sense of detachment. In both cases, these premises advance the idea that migrants—especially ones of color—suffer some form of social and economic inequity in the institutions and structures of their settlement states (Siu, 2001). In contrast, Latin American scholars and sociologists Renato Rosaldo (1997) and William Flores and Rina Benmayor (1997) claim that cultural citizenship is the genesis of positive civil and social advancement that defines the type of place-making that occurs within Latin American immigrant social clubs. These organizations celebrate homeland norms and values while promoting settlement political and economic empowerment. The investigation phase in Miami added weight to two arguments advanced in chapter 2: (1) many first-generation Ecuadorian migrant acculturations are also heavily influenced by personal and private interracial or interethnic relationships, and (2) these collaborations formed by them shape their lives inside and outside the social club network. The most salient characteristic of Ecuadorian migrants shared by many of the Miami subjects of this study is their feeling and demonstration of having achieved a high level of personal social and economic success. An analysis of the shared goals of two clubs and a focus on key members of these organizations sheds light on the individual conflicts involved in attaining the American Dream as this quest intersects with the idea of living a "good life."

The Miami findings add weight to Ran Abramitzky and Lean Boustan's (2017, 1326) assertion about migration: after approximately 10 years, immigrants arriving with advanced skill sets rapidly catch up and are able to overtake the economic achievements of natives. Although the informants did not directly speak of their paths to success as double-consciousness experiences, they are members of the transnational mass of refugees that sociologist Peggy Levitt (2003) refers to as migrants with "feet in both worlds." As such, they have suffered and feared being victimized and racialized because of global apartheid in two geographical places (180). This research found that Miami's Ecuadorian immigrants who are members of social organizations overcome the forces of transnational racialization by pursuing local and global altruistic projects. This book's focus on success responds to Max Planck Institute anthropologist Steven Vertovec's (2009, 19) call for more scholarship about different socioeconomic groups of immigrants. The Miami part of the study accomplishes this by calling attention to the relationships and circumstances that shaped and framed Ecuadorian immigration journeys in two very different social clubs: the food pantry and community outreach organization known as Vecinos en Acción (Neighbors in Action) and the socially engaged organization Liga Ecuatoriana de Florida (Ecuadorian League [Union] of Florida).

Vecinos en Acción

In 2015, I found the number of Ecuadorian social organizations listed throughout Florida to be less than 15. Most were affiliated with charitable organizations in the United States (the Ecuadorian Lions Club, the Ecuadorian Red Cross, the Ecuadorian American Chamber of Commerce of Miami, etc.). Several reflected in their names the membership's involvement in the Federation of International Employers, a multinational human resource alliance. Vecinos en Acción was one of only two Ecuadorian migrant associations in Florida dedicated to community and transnational philanthropic outreach.

Vecinos's offices are in a small warehouse facility, most of whose footprint is devoted to housing a food pantry. The building sets back about 50 feet from the curb on a hectic one-way street, and the entrance to the pantry is a garage door with vertical plastic shutters. According to the family who control this organization, Vecinos and a church-based pantry are the only two charitable organizations in East Little Havana. There is a severe scarcity of critical resources for the poor in Little Havana, which for decades has been the initial settlement zone for successive waves of nationally diverse Latin Americans who in many cases lack the preparation and resources needed to survive their settlement into Miami's social hierarchy.

Vecinos's 25 years of success in meeting the subsistence needs of Little Havana's and Miami's multiethnic poor population is no small accomplishment. This study's participants agreed that the city of Miami traditionally invests very little in supporting the settlement of Latin American migrants. This is especially true for those who share two characteristics: regionalized enunciation of Spanish that differs from the dominant Cuban accent and features that are non-White or not of White Cuban descent. This study found a third category of distinction that is reinforced to some extent within the social clubs: class difference. Although extant scholarship argues that a good education does not guarantee social mobility (Aja et al., 2019), membership in a successful class in Miami is at least in part based on migratory preparedness and the ability to gain access to the better jobs controlled by the city's Whites and Cuban elites. As non-Cubans, Ecuadorian migrants face two challenges. The first obstacle is to establish cultural citizenship and thereby acquire the social capital necessary to compete for work outside the informal labor force.

A second hurdle is finding a pathway to professional jobs while working for low wages and waiting years to validate their homeland credentials. Only after accreditation will they be able to secure lucrative employment in Florida's tourist-based and international trade industries. During what can be a long transition to a professional level of employment, many of the informants were quite poor. This project found that this situation adversely affects the social clubs because low-wage earners lack the disposable income needed to pay club membership dues. For the same reason, workers who are paid low wages or non-wage – those that receive a set rate per year no matter how much they work, a category that comprises the majority of Miami's Latin American population, can't afford to attend events sponsored by these organizations.

Three members of the family who founded and still run Vecinos en Acción contributed interviews to this research: Laura, an Ecuadorian immigrant; her husband Fernando, who migrated to Miami from Cuba in the 1960s; and their son Ronald, a second-generation Ecuadorian-Cuban who now resides in New York City. Ronald's insightful testimony about Miami's complex multiethnic and shifting hegemonic social order appears in this book's first chapter. Laura, Fernando, and their youngest son Ricky spend countless hours at Vecinos en Acción, and Ronald and his new wife also volunteer their time to the organization whenever they visit Miami. Running Vecinos en Acción fulfills the personal place-making objectives of Laura, the family matriarch. For Laura, who struggled as an unaccepted "poor" Ecuadorian in Miami's class-based society, Vecinos en Acción represents a safe harbor where she can be of service to the multiethnic underpaid and sometimes homeless majority of Miami's citizens. Fernando, Laura's Cuban-born husband, views Vecinos as the place where he is able to shape what is for him the end result of achieving the American Dream, a "good life."

Laura was born in 1953 in Guayaquil. When she was barely 17 years old, she left alone for Miami. Her plans over the years have not changed much: Laura dreams of being able to expand the pantry legacy of service to uplift Miami's less fortunate and her family. According to Laura, her mother was in charge of raising the children and maintaining the household, while her father, who was in the military, supervised everything outside the home. Laura feels her childhood was not typical because she accompanied her mother on outreach missions to serve the poor throughout Ecuador. Laura describes herself as different from other migrants because she left Ecuador to be of service to others rather than to follow a dream of material success. She spoke warmly of the cultural diversity she saw while accompanying her mother on missionary field trips, and she expressed her discomfort that dissimilarities between people are too often used as reasons to divide and mistreat the less fortunate. According to Laura, her mother, like her grandmother before her, practiced giving as a way to ensure the well-being of all of their neighbors. For this reason, Laura claims she was shown by example that there is no justifiable reason to distinguish among people based on skin color or the ways they celebrate their cultures. Her mother helped everyone, no matter their race, ethnicity, class, or gender. At the same time, Laura's mother emphasized education and protected the unity and solidarity of the family unit by forbidding Laura and her siblings from playing with other kids who were not members of the immediate family.

Because of her strict upbringing and isolation within the family, Laura refers to her brothers and sisters as lifelong friends. In fact, the bonds they share are the reasons she feels at home, "en casa," when she returns at least twice a year to visit in Ecuador. When I asked if her many Ecuadorian cousins and her brothers and sister believe she has been changed by her experiences in the United States, Laura said, "I feel *en casa* because we sit around reminiscing about the old times. They treat me well, even though they notice my accent, my accent because my husband is Cuban, and I've lived in Miami with so many Cubans that my accent has changed. I feel like a citizen in the middle" (Laura, 2016).

Laura's marriage in 1973 may have resulted in a change in the way she speaks Spanish, but she self-identifies as White (blanca) in both Ecuador and the United States. Laura is legally a citizen of Ecuador and the United States, and her continued dedication to altruistic principles through Vecinos en Acción (Figure 9 Miami Laura Pantry) support her contention that she is a productive citizen, or member, of a space between her homeland and her settlement country. For Laura, the idea of accomplishing the American Dream is conflated with constructing a good life: "Being American

Figure 9. (Left to right)
A client, Laura
and her son Ricky

is part of my life. I spent my adulthood in the United States. Here in Miami, I never experienced discrimination. . . . Everyone treated me in good spirit. It's because I have relationships with positive people here [Miami], people who give me love and supported me. They are my wall against discrimination. . . . They've made my life easier, happier" (Laura, 2016). Safety and having the freedom or ability to act on her desire to serve are Laura's primary objectives. She does not deny that there is racial, gender, or class bias in Miami. Instead, she revealed that she established a buffer or multiethnic support network of individuals outside her family that she feels protected her from discrimination and supported her efforts to grow Vecinos en Acción.

Regarding the opportunities and good fortune that some Ecuadorian immigrants I interviewed for this research have found in the United States, Laura said that many others fail because they lack proper immigration documents, have skill sets that are not in demand, and have less than high school educations. According to Laura, some fear a homeland return and prefer living in poverty in the United States. Countless others are unwilling to survive on several meager service-sector jobs. Despite the disgrace of returning to the homeland, which is well documented by Pribilsky's (2007) research, they sometimes do exercise this option. Does this difficult set of circumstances incentivize Ecuadorian migrants to seek help from agencies like Vecinos?

Laura noted that over the years few Ecuadorian migrants have reached out for assistance from Vecinos. She believes that Ecuadorians do not want to be seen as in need of help. "I see this even in Ecuador, when we go there to deliver aid. They are reluctant to step forward and ask" (Laura, 2016). In the United States, migrants in general stay in the shadows to avoid encounters with ICE. This climate of fear reduces the number of migrants who come to Ecuadorian functions and facilities. Another factor is that most Miami community outreach organizations like Vecinos en Acción are run by higher-wage-earning immigrants. Sociologist Richard Benton (2016, 209) explores the complexities of this possibility to explain the absence of migrants at Vecinos en Acción. Benton finds a strong likelihood that "lower status individuals also tend to have weaker relationships with high status contacts." In this case, a class barrier is created against accepting and understanding altruistic acts on the part of social organizations. This class-based obstacle could also prevent lower-wage earners from developing a better understanding of charitable resource distribution and the benefits of gaining social capital and a sense of empowerment indigenous to ethnic social clubs (209).

After the doors of Vecinos en Acción opened in the late 1980s, Laura and Fernando established a policy of only soliciting and accepting funding from private sources. There are two reasons for their decision: (1) too many prejudiced government elites make grant-funding decisions that reflect popular and discriminatory ideas about skin complexion and Spanish or English proficiency, and (2) the expensive and excessive accountability process that federal and state funders demand can actually deplete resources. This erosion of revenues can take a toll on the food pantry's most valuable asset: its volunteer labor force. According to Fernando, this type of drain on the coffers and rigid oversight of Vecinos en Acción defeats the purpose of the organization to serve Miami's multiethnic homeless and help immigrants who may be undocumented and/or unable to work and sustain their families.

Vecinos en Acción traditionally maintains a flexible community service agenda. For this reason, the types of public support the foundation provides have changed over the years. The objective has always been to meet the policy demands of the city while providing an assortment of necessities and services to continuous waves of nationally different migratory populations. Vecinos in the past has hosted a citywide sports league, assisted girls with high-risk pregnancies, and even provided basic educational guidance. But, over the past 25 years, the family sometimes has found itself at odds with high-ranking bureaucrats. According to Fernando, the same officials who publicly showered Laura with honors at the same time diligently created policies that advanced the racialization of non-Whites and non-Cubans. Enforcement of these unjust policies repeatedly required the family to shut down vital programs. The result was that many city-sponsored outreach projects failed to consistently prevent the growth of an underprepared "lower-class" population of migrants in Miami. This type of hegemonic control by the government also constrains the transnational giving practices of Vecinos en Acción.

According to Fernando, the corruption of government officials and the military in Ecuador grossly complicates the logistics Vecinos en Acción has to deal with to deliver resources to impoverished women and children in Ecuadorian villages. Fernando and Laura always travel alone and without protection while in Ecuador. They do this to personally protect their goods and to make sure they actually reach the villagers in need in remote regions. Along the way the national and provincial governments demand fees for valueless permits that in the end provide no security for what Fernando described as a very dangerous journey.

Each time they deliver resources the number of bureaucratic barriers increase, making the experience of giving back to Laura's homeland often frustrating. Once they reach their destination, the villagers frequently view them with suspicion and often even refuse to accept the aid. I asked Fernando—and later Laura—if the villagers were under any type of duress and if their refusal of aid could be a response to a social or physical threat. Fernando and Laura indicated that although their project was politically discouraged by regional, local, and national authorities, they saw no evidence of coercion by these outside forces that would intimidate the villagers or persuade them to refuse aid. On a few occasions, hesitant villagers talked with Laura and Fernando about these instances of refusal. Some informants mentioned a cultural belief in the villages that attached a sense of personal shame and failure to accepting help—no matter how badly it is needed. Laura and Fernando agreed that the ambivalent behavior of the villagers in Ecuador—and the reluctance of Ecuadorians in Miami to seek help from social agencies like Vecinos en Acción—are related. In this way, the couple brought some clarity to why many U.S.-settled Ecuadorians may resist family and especially outside assistance.

The tendency of Ecuadorians to place so much value on self-sufficiency slowly emerged in the research as one of the reasons for a decline in social club membership. Black feminist sociologist Patricia Hill Collins (2002, 117) persuasively argues that there is a strong correlation between financial self-sufficiency and self-reliance. Although Collins's focus was on the behavior of Afro-American females, her analysis opens the door to considering the relevance of expressions of self-sufficiency by other double-consciousness individuals. Viewing self-sufficiency through the lens of financial independence gives meaning to testimonies in all three field sites about the impact of job loss and economic instability. Individuals experiencing declining income spoke about their failure to attain the American Dream. In most cases, the subjects felt that they had prepared themselves educationally to immigrate. But despite their level of preparedness, without financial independence, they expressed feelings of estrangement—especially from social club members they considered to be successful.

Fernando insisted on a key idea that relates to preparedness. He claimed that education is a means to achieve the American Dream, which opened for him the door to create a good life in the United States. His assertion about the value of education to the migratory experience is substantiated by several contemporary writers, including Chicano studies scholar Leisy Abrego (2014) in her work on Salvadoran settlement. Anthropologist Ana Zentella's (1997) linguistic ethnography about Puerto Rican migrants, and sociologist Tiffany Joseph's investigation of Brazilian settlement in New York City also add weight to this basic idea that acculturation is facilitated by enhancing the skill sets migrants bring from the homeland. Miami informants spoke about their high investment in education and, as with most Latin Americans immigrants in related studies, their goals included earning college degrees and helping their children to do the same. Their dedication to self-improvement is reflected the fact that Miami was ranked in 2015 as the number one U.S. city for Latino college educational achievement. Education is shown in this way to be related to community involvement or what Portes et al. (2007, 254) refer to as "participation in transnational activities—economic, political, and cultural." My research also found a relationship among education, the hierarchal class divide in Miami, and the rapid decline in membership of the city's most active Latino social club, La Liga Ecuatoriana de Florida.

La Liga Ecuatoriana de Florida

Founded in 1980, La Liga Ecuatoriana de Florida (La Liga) is headquartered in a warehouse district of Kendall, about 24 miles west of downtown Miami. Unlike Ecuadorian clubs in Los Angeles and New York, La Liga does not come together to host an annual parade or festival. Also, the appointment of a queen each year and the charitable transnational activities that this event fosters are both activities solely sponsored and exclusively managed by La Liga members. Membership access to La Liga for non-native born Ecuadorians is limited to special events, and the club does not have a food pantry or offices housing acculturation training programs for either the documented or undocumented. Guests at club events are not asked about their immigration status, and La Liga is for the most part a nonpolitical organization. Provisions of the club's bylaws require outside groups and individuals in both Ecuador and Miami to petition by application to receive funding, except in the case of a dire emergency. An example of an emergency is the need for support created by a natural disaster. Then–La Liga president José paraphrased what he thought to be La Liga's mission: to be of service to others in Ecuador and Miami. José believed the club's most pressing concern to be recruiting and keeping the interest of younger members. What follows is an exploration of the possible reasons Ecuadorian immigrant participation in clubs is declining.

Figure 10. La Liga Ecuatoriana—1st floor main room.

Figure 11. (Left to right behind the bar) Susanna's husband, José's wife ("la Colombiana"), Susanna, and a guest at the event.

The field study at La Liga included my 2015 attendance at an event after the eruption of the usually dormant volcano Cotopaxi. This natural disaster elicited a widespread but uncoordinated response from Ecuadorian social clubs throughout the United States. Each association acting independently held community events at which they invited all Latin Americans to raise disaster relief funds for the homeland. Over the next few months, clubs like La Liga purchased subsistence supplies, and the members decided where in the homeland their club would ship goods. The supply chain for most of the organizations terminated in an Ecuadorian province or region with which the club already had established lines of communication and a history of supplying prior services to the local population. A lack of a desire to merge for a common cause is related to two observations I have already advanced. First, Ecuadorian homeland ideas about geographical and ethnic differences can restrict network formation in the settlement nation. Second, what feminist theorist refer to as social capital—the gain of "mutual benefits" by individuals who share norms, trust, and values within family and community networks (Zambrana & Zoppi, 2002)—makes it culturally normal for Ecuadorians to extend trust to strangers slowly. Collaboration with other organizations and the recruitment of new members by Ecuadorian clubs is both the building of a trust relationship and the construction of social capital. I raised these two points as possible issues affecting La Liga membership expansion when I met with then–La Liga president José.

José. Class Difference, Collaboration and Growth

José, who has only one sibling, a sister, was born in 1972 in Guayaquil. He and his wife—a Colombian immigrant—are currently applying for U.S. citizenship. He plans to also obtain dual citizenship for himself and his children, who were both born in the United States. José self-identifies in Ecuador and the United States as White or *blanco*, although he suspects that there may be Indigenous blood in his family tree. When I asked him to elaborate about his claim to Whiteness, José's reply revealed what he thinks about the practice of racializing culture in both the United States and Ecuador: "In Ecuador, I'd say I'm White, it's just because that's the way I've been identifying myself all my life. It makes more sense. When they just say Hispanic in the U.S., they don't differentiate, even though some places they put Hispanic and under that they'll have different classifications—I haven't paid much attention because race to me is not a big thing. I know though that culture is a big deal. Mom and Dad did not dwell on things like race, even though in a place like Ecuador where you are immersed in different cultures and racial distinction is so vivid, it gets in your veins. . . . There I too made ugly racial jokes that I today would consider profiling" (José, 2016).

José claims that in Ecuador class was more of an issue during his youth than race and gender. His Ecuadorian family made every attempt to reduce the impact of their class difference by acquiring all the bells and whistles that marked them as members of the middle class; they employed more than one maid, and José had a *nana*, or nanny. Regarding racial difference, José admits to having strong and biased opinions when he lived in Ecuador. Since he settled in Miami in 2000, José's broad network of business associates are both culturally and what he considers to be racially diverse. He did, however, express a great deal of apprehension about establishing relationships with Afro-Americans. According to José, for no apparent reason, Afro-Americans sometimes convey what he feels is undeserved hostility toward him and others who appear to be White. Despite this, he insisted that his homeland-based viewpoints have been changed because of his lived experiences as a migrant. I pursued the issues of race and class across gender lines when I interviewed former La Liga president Cecilia.

Cecilia. Beauty and Transnational Community

Cecilia claimed Indigenous and Afro blood during the part of her interview session when we discussed race and ethnicity in Ecuador. She was emphatic that there is no White or European blood in her family. After several minutes of deep thought, she identified as mestiza based on phenotypical characteristics she has seen in her grandmother. As she examined the ethnic categories in the latest Ecuadorian census, she at first thought the available classifications actually posited Whiteness at the top of the list and darker colors by shade at different levels at the bottom. If true, this would create an economic hierarchy and not one based on ethnicity. This conflation of race and class, which speaks to the racialization process in the Ecuador, also appeared to influence her opinion about labels such as *Hispanic* and *Latino/a* used to describe Latin Americans in the U.S. census. Regarding her identity in the United States, she expressed concern that the term *Hispanic* is a racialized expression—or, in her words, "a term that provides justification to direct prejudice toward certain people . . . to group all Latin Americans together without any regard for the diversity of their cultures" (Cecilia, 2016).

For Cecilia, dividing people into different classes has caused the most damage to members of the lowest class in both Ecuador and the United States. Cecilia and I discussed the concept of "the good life." She said that although her father had gone above and beyond the call of duty to support his employees and one of his sisters, she had never seen either of her parents devote time to serving the community. She explains, "After moving here at age 24 [to Miami in 1984], I went back to Ecuador for the first time and to have servants bothered me. . . . They seemed like slaves. . . . People can't get up and get their own glass of water. Here the American Dream is obviously to have your house, your family, your pet, live in a very comfortable way, not be rich . . . just to have your family and a place you call a home—that's the American Dream, we had something similar over there [Ecuador]" (Cecilia, 2016).

Cecilia's claims to success include the accomplishments of her two daughters, who both graduated from college, and her ability to care for her 83-year-old mother, in which she recognizes she is very fortunate. Like Laura, Cecilia is married to a Cuban, but the similarities appear to end at this point. Their viewpoints about placemaking or acculturation reflect their distinct involvements in the varied cultural climates in two very different social clubs.

As early as 1975 while living in New York City, Cecilia served in multiple roles, as either a candidate, an elected queen, or an event organizer for social club competitions. She enjoyed the spotlight, but she did not become a very active member of the organizations in New York. However, after moving to Florida she gained citywide notoriety as Miami's Latin American Queen of Queens. As her popularity increased, so did her interest in the business side of producing and managing the pageants. According to Cecilia, she became devoted to improving the process of electing the queens and attracting more interethnic Latin American support in Miami. Another benefit was that she noticed while doing this work that other national Latino groups were disjointed and not formally organized in the same way as La Liga. Her work with the pageant also showed her that she could help the event grow. Each year there are now two citywide, multination Latin American contests. The history of the pageants reflects Miami's multiethnic past: "We now have up to 25 participants, 2 per country. . . . Nicaraguans win the most . . . but, when the populations in Miami change, so does the nationality of the winners. For example, the Brazilians won a lot. . . . Then, at one time there were a lot of wealthy people here from Latin America and the girls looked German, when all the wealthy people left, then other groups started to win. . . . They are the descendants of first-generation Latin American migrants" (Cecilia, 2016).

After winning pageants and accomplishing many of the goals she set for herself as a project director, Cecilia accepted the invitation in the early 1990s to become a La Liga board member. Under her leadership as president in 1999, La Liga obtained a 501(c)(3) federal nonprofit classification. Because of her high visibility throughout Miami, Cecilia has been able to establish a broad network of political influence that includes the U.S. Ecuadorian consulates, international corporations, and the Ecuadorian Ministry. Unfortunately, her reign as the leader of La Liga also exposed her to personal abuse from men accustomed to domination.

There were many occasions when Cecilia had to prove she would not succumb or relinquish control to the misogynistic practices exercised by males inside and outside La Liga. According to Cecilia, the passive aggressiveness of fellow club members was no more than an attempt by male members to belittle her husband personally and her contributions to the organization. Latinx scholarship about Mexican migration (Castañeda & Zavella, 2003) and recent studies of the psychosocial impact of homeland beliefs and practices (Falicov, 2017) provide evidence that psychological abuse is one aspect of machismo that crosses international borders during the migratory process. The insulters demanded that she act more "feminine or submissive. But I told them this is not Ecuador. No, I wouldn't put up with them [males] who didn't even respect me after I married" (Cecilia, 2016). Cecilia explained that this, to her, was really a powerful act of disrespect intended to belittle and emasculate her husband. Despite these demonstrations of hegemonic masculinity, and the opposition she sometimes encounters in part because she is a woman, Cecilia finds many reasons to continue to serve on the board. She spoke of the joy she feels each time she travels with the Queen to Ecuador to distribute La Liga's gifts to the poor. "Liga became first my job then my family, my family should have been first, then job, then family. . . . I had to make sure La Liga's name was at the top, that all the directors helped me to help the people in Ecuador" (Cecilia, 2016).

José and I discussed La Liga's economic and political engagements in Ecuador and the local community. He began by emphatically stating that as far as the U.S. and Ecuadorian governments are concerned, La Liga is a federally registered 501(c)(3) nonprofit and nonpolitical foundation: "We're community activists. La Liga doesn't have anything to do with this current government, it's just the policy of the institution. We represent [Ecuadorians]. Getting a stain is so easy; scraping off the stain not so easy" (José, 2016). By referring to the possible effects of forming political alliances outside the organization as staining, José made it clear that La Liga's purpose for the past 35 years has been to create a welcoming space in the local Miami community and to provide specific services to other Ecuadorians across global borders.

As Cecilia and I walked out of the salon, I noticed that she drove a late-model luxury car. Like many of the members of La Liga, José also drives a very attractive late-model luxury car. Could it be possible that these opulent displays of success discouraged less fortunate Ecuadorian immigrants from attending events? For this reason, I next discussed the issue of affordability as a factor in both membership and event attendance. After all, roundtrip via Uber to La Liga from my apartment in Little Havana cost $40, admission each night to an event cost $20, and a plate of food without a drink was between $5 and $7. I asked José what was the cost of belonging to La Liga and whether he felt people who might want to join could not afford it. He responded, "We have now about 80 subscribers/members who get a discount to events at the door, at a cost of $75 for a family and for individuals $60 a year. Right now, you have to be Ecuadorian to join, but with Ecuadorians marrying other people, this will I hope change. I believe taking Uber to get here is reasonable, the cost of drinks between $1 and $15, maybe they'd spend $100 in any other Miami location for an event like this. So the cost to attend is average for Miami" (José, 2016).

José reflected on the differences in perceptions of affordability and the reality of class membership in Miami. The ambitions José expressed are grounded in the reality that the numbers of Ecuadorians migrating to Miami has sharply decreased, while relationships between existing migrants from Ecuador and other ethnic and Latin American national groups are greatly increasing. José's comment also reveals a need to expand La Liga's mission to accommodate less-fortunate Latin Americans living in Miami. According to 2017 U.S. Census projections about the level of poverty in Miami by ethnicity, 40% of Hispanics live below the poverty line. A geographical assessment of immigrant employment by S. Carter Christopher and Timothy F. Leslie (2014, 177) demonstrates that in Miami's Cuban-dominated marketplace, small migrant populations such as Ecuadorians need social capital networks like La Liga to support their advancement in the labor market.

Two questions emerged from the research phase at La Liga: First, what could a deeper and more prolonged immersion into the daily operations at La Liga reveal about the multi–Latin American tapestry of Miami? Second, how will this cultural dynamic influence José's dream for the club to increase the number of younger Ecuadorian immigrants? The analysis of race advanced by sociologist Eduardo Bonilla-Silva and this study's participant Ronald sheds some light on these issues: race is a social construct that influences place-making in a color-blind U.S. society. The way Ecuadorian clubs continue to practice place-making in the future will be framed and shaped by two conditions: (1) Ecuadorian migration to the United States is decreasing, and (2) as my interview subjects suggested, there is an accompanying rise in the number of interethnic marriages involving U.S. Ecuadorian immigrants already settled in Miami. In New York City, the turbulent history of Latin American migrants' acculturation into a culturally diverse social climate extends over a much longer period than in Los Angeles or Miami, nearly 400 years. The next phase of research explored place-making in New York and the light it can shed on the impact of time on the processes of interethnic social change and Ecuadorian migrant acculturation.

Chapter 4

Class and Advancement: New York City's Ecuadorian Civic Committee Nueva York in Corona (Queens) and New Paradigms Keeping Themselves

The New York City phase of research presented another cultural context to explore issues of acculturation previously examined in Los Angeles and Miami. As with organizations in the first two cities, I evaluated the organizational history of the Ecuadorian Civic Committee Nueva York (ECCNY) with the recognition that the club's role as a place of identity-making is related to the lived experiences of key members. I sought to expand on Pribilsky's (2007) observation that working-class Ecuadorian migrants—especially the undocumented—feel estranged from more settled and successful club members. Pribilsky brings this issue forward when mentioning the local and transnational altruistic and political missions of New York City's Ecuadorian social organizations. This chapter's more nuanced analysis of ECCNY provides a window on the past 30 years of one of the city's Ecuadorian social clubs. In this book as a whole, the ECCNY research also serves as a bridge to discuss new Ecuadorian migrant paradigms of self-expression and service rapidly emerging outside the network of existing social clubs.

In 2015, New York City's Ecuadorian migrant club with the highest internet visibility was the Ecuadorian International Center (EIC) in Jackson Heights. EIC's website features a list of special services it offers to the community, including English, citizenship preparation, professional workplace training, and General Educational Development (GED) classes. EIC was established in 1999, almost a decade later than many of the associations featured in this study. When I conducted field site research in 2015, EIC's online publicity about their services featured legal assistance and job-training opportunities for 9/11 victims, Deferred Action for Childhood Arrivals (DACA) applicants and recipients, and multinational immigrants—with no mention of a required migration status. The group's humanitarian mission emphasized a goal to prepare a pathway for those in need to be able to enjoy a sense of equality in the workplace and U.S. society. EIC's publicly expressed role to provide a space of political empowerment for the double-consciousness migrant sets it apart from the more passive organizations I studied in Los Angeles and Miami.

I found engagement in politics to resist the oppression and marginalization of global apartheid to be a shared characteristic of New York City's Ecuadorian organizations. Another philanthropic community project was underway in 2015 under the banner of the Queens Ecuadorian International Center. Founded in 2006, Organización Juventud Ecuatoriana (JUVE, Ecuadorian Youth Organization) is a place-making empowerment model. JUVE's outreach efforts specifically focus on achieving individual mobility through higher education, the development of Latin American pride, and the creation of strong and supportive global networks of settlement and homeland populations. JUVE cultivates leadership in migrants of Ecuadorian heritage by way of a generous scholarship. JUVE and EIC represent a postmillennium approach by Ecuadorian organizations to undertake projects pursuing social justice. ECCNY became the New York case study because its founding date of 1980 is similar to the establishment dates of the previously explored Miami and Los Angeles organizations.

The ECCNY offices in Corona are on the second floor at the end of a narrow hallway, in a suite of rooms overlooking a small shopping area. When I arrived, the office space was full of donations being staged for shipment for earthquake victims in Ecuador. The walls were decorated with photos and memorabilia featuring then-president Oswaldo in the company of Ecuadorian and U.S. dignitaries.

Oswaldo claimed mestizo identity in Ecuador based on a combined Indigenous and *blanco* (White) heritage. In the United States, he selected *español* (Spanish or from Spain) as an ethnicity and White as a race. He contextualized Whiteness by saying that in the United States, *blanco* means a person who is not of Indian or Afro ancestry. In 1969, Oswaldo arrived in New York City from his hometown near Quito in the sierra with a degree in psychology and the dream of becoming a college professor. He immediately began to establish a network of friends, including an Argentinian and other Ecuadorians, who helped him as he searched for work and improved his English. The network's support enabled Oswaldo's efforts to acculturate as he advanced from a menial job in the garment industry to the position from which he recently retired as a dealer of blue list stocks on Wall Street. According to Oswaldo, this lucrative career enabled him to attain the American Dream.

Oswaldo showed me a magazine with many pictures of very well-educated and successful Ecuadorian immigrants. He indicated that professionalism, or the achievement of a level of education that will support the challenge of achieving the American Dream, is still an objective being pursued by immigrants from Ecuador. I also asked Oswaldo about the current participation of Ecuadorian immigrants as members or clients in ECCNY. Although he described the majority as economically and educationally disadvantaged, he did indicate that providing service for the documented and undocumented was a goal of the organization. Regarding Ecuadorian participation in both immigration categories as members or guests, Ecuador's migrant population tended to avoid ECCNY. "We don't see them [Ecuadorian immigrants] here much. They are scattered all over New York and many are undocumented and afraid. . . . We don't ask about your [immigration] status here, and we are holding English classes for migrants and welcome Latin Americans from any country. Ecuadorian immigrants that enter and are known by the consulate do hear about us, . . . but many others focus on caring for their families" (Oswaldo, 2016).

Census estimates published by the Pew Research Group have indicated that the population of Ecuadorian migrants in the United States is less than 700,000. Oswaldo strongly disagreed, saying this figure in no way reflects the reality that there are probably at least 1 million immigrants currently settled in the greater New York City area alone. He provided insightful and firsthand observations about work and living conditions for Ecuadorians migrants in the city. For the most part, Ecuadorians are undocumented workers who protect their ability to remain in the United States by avoiding contact with all U.S. and Ecuadorian authorities and organizations. He described the socioeconomic conditions of most Ecuadorians in New York. "Very few succeed here, less than 30%. The lack of work opportunities in the United States force them to return to Ecuador—heavily in debt in most cases. Here, most work construction, where they have little opportunity to improve themselves. . . . These are not professionals. They live in apartments, some work in factories and restaurants . . . doing whatever they have to do to care for their families—including their families back in Ecuador" (Oswaldo, 2016).

ECCNY's 501(c)(3) federal status as a nonprofit organization allows it to raise funds and distribute various types of support in the United States and Ecuador. The foundation has a small school in Ecuador's highlands near Quito, where it maintains a facility for children who need eyeglasses. This school-based eye program charges US$3.00 to check vision. Patients arrive at the facility from all Ecuadorian regions. The distribution of funding in the homeland is accompanied by an outreach program in the United States. At the ECCNY facility, an English-language program for immigrants from many Latin American nations fosters place-making empowerment.

Leonor, ECCNY's event director, is from the sierra province of Azuay and self-identifies as mestizo in Ecuador. She finds the U.S. concepts of race and ethnic identity confusing. Once again, context dictates identity construction in the settlement nation. As the darkest member of the household, her family refers to her as "negra" (Black), and she checks "native" (Native American) on job applications to correspond to her claimed identity in the homeland. Leonor is both a benefactor and facilitator of the cultural citizenship fostered by ECCNY place-making construction projects. She completed high school in Ecuador and arrived in the United States with a marketable skill set. She employed her talents as a seamstress in a New Jersey factory. Over the next 13 years, Leonor completed several language and educational enrichment programs that resulted in the company's sponsoring her green card application.

Leonor's double-consciousness experiences include deportation, reentry to the United States, and the acquisition of dual U.S. and Ecuadorian citizenship. Her immigration is a chronicle of the impact of transnational capital on immigrant acculturation in New York City. "I came without papers. In '84, they were going into the factory, and I had a very bad experience there. It was very hard then . . . undocumented. If you didn't have papers at that time, then, if you didn't speak English . . . you had to start working in the restaurants. We [she and her husband] had to leave, then [when] we came back the garment industry was not paying well, no big manufacturing companies, just making samples to send out to manufactures . . . which was being done overseas. Now, the designer's interns are being used to do even that work—now, there are a lot of students from Colombia, many being used to do this type of work" (Leonor, 2015). Like many of the subjects of this study in all three locations, for Leonor multiethnic networking and the increased mobility that accompanies citizenship enabled her to accomplish the goal cited in the first chapter by Anonymous, "keep yourself." Leonor embodies keeping yourself and refers to herself as a successful individual with a strong social network, or in her words, an "Ecua-U.S.A. citizen capable of constructing opportunities for myself and others who really need it" (Leonor, 2015). This study found evidence that across geographical settlement contexts, the Ecuadorian immigrant desire to keep oneself is a sense of belonging facilitated by club membership.

Regarding organizational participation, during the 1990s all three research areas experienced accelerated metropolitan expansion and industrial shifts favoring migrants with high levels of premigratory preparation. Traditional Latin American immigrant neighborhoods began to dissolve as did the memberships of many of the social organizations in these communities. Another problem began to emerge during this same time period. For decades, the objective of achieving the American Dream served to unite club members. As the evidence in this study shows, long-term settlers who had achieved success were again united when they started to question the values of this capitalistic ideal. Another dynamic exacerbated the decline in the appeal of this notion of achievement. Migrants from Ecuador after the turn of the new century arrived with ideas deeply rooted in a homeland rise in anti-neoliberalism. Many members of the postmillennium wave were dissatisfied with austerity politics that ignored human suffering—especially migrants who claimed to be members of the Indigenous, *montubio*, and Afro-Ecuadorian populations. The identity politics of post-2000 Ecuador encouraged civil engagement and a type of political politics that turned away from the blanket materialistic quest to achieve the American Dream. The next case studies address an associated question: Is it possible to construct a sense of belonging to promote mobility and empowerment outside the network of existing Ecuadorian social clubs?

New Paradigms beyond Geographic Boundaries

The social entrepreneurs advancing new paradigms to promote the development of a strong sense of belonging among Ecuadorian migrants have two common characteristics: the goal of encouraging cultural citizenship and a desire, shared with the club members, to construct a good life. These individuals' efforts to bring about unity operate outside the formalized boundaries of existing Ecuadorian social clubs. Place-making experiences and the creation of new solidarity paradigms is a progressive expression of Ecuadorian immigrant acculturation. The common feature of these new models and the traditional social clubs is their use of approaches to developing cultural citizenship that may or may not involve political activism. These characteristics, stressed throughout this book, include network creation across ethnic boundaries and the promotion and improvement of their own talents as members of successful settlement classes.

As a part of this research, I compiled a list of 30 migrants from Ecuador who are professional artists. The sample group members tend to live in large metropolitan areas and work independently: when I asked 10 subjects in Los Angeles, Miami, and New York City if they personally knew their fellow countrymen on this list, the answer was usually no. These artists include well-established and often award-winning vocalists like Joe Arroyo and Ricardo Arjona and pianist Hugo Realpe. The musical performers on the list do have one thing in common: they all rely heavily on the professional services of a small group of Ecuadorian immigrant event managers—like the next interviewee, Danny Daniel—to coordinate their bookings in the Ecuadorian club network.

Danny Daniel: Entertaining and Giving

Danny does not claim Ecuadorian citizenship. He studied the Ecuadorian 2010 census and self-identified as *montubio*, a choice from the homeland that leads him to believe that he is an Afro-American citizen in the United States. Danny struggled with both questions regarding ethnicity on the 2010 U.S. Census and concluded, "I don't consider myself Hispanic—that's not a race, and I'm not White or African. Choosing 'other' makes me feel like a second-rate citizen" (Danny, 2016). Although Danny claimed to be extremely proud of his African heritage and referred to his childhood in Ecuador as happy, he remembers being shunned in Ecuador as a *montubio*. According to Danny, his feelings of shame relate to the severe social stratification disfavoring people of Afro heritage that existed during his childhood in the provinces of Monta and Manabí. The performers Danny represents are from many Latin American nationalities and ethnicities. Danny is one of the managers in a non-cohesive group of Ecuadorian migrants who specialize in booking Ecuadorian artists and talent from other Latin American countries in Miami and New York. He travels the East Coast, and it is not uncommon for him to perform sessions accompanying his clients.

The story of Danny's settlement in New York City is made more complex by the fact that his parents were an interracial couple. Community customs and legal mandates tied to the couple's racial differences forced them to flee their ancestral coastal province of Monta. While in hiding, they decided in the late 1960s that the father would migrate first to the United States. In 1970, the entire family followed and settled in Ozone Park, Queens. At that time, this now-gentrified community was heavily populated by Ecuadorian settlers. In 1978, a sudden reduction in income resulted in the family's return to Ecuador. Danny grew up in Monta and later Puerto Viejo. In these small towns, he began to prepare a professional set of skills that would be useful to his reentry in the United States. While still in the homeland, Danny attended Catholic high school, elevated his level of Spanish proficiency, took piano lessons, and learned to play guitar. During these early years in the homeland, Danny's disc jockey experiences with fellow musicians led to the discovery of his talent for organizing and promoting groups.

Ecuador's precarious economics played a key role in prompting the family to once again enter the transnational migratory circuit. His mother, a skilled seamstress, heard through her global network of friends about employment opportunities at a tie factory in New York. Now divorced, she led the family's migration back to the United States in 1987. As a non–English speaker, and dependent on the earnings of only his mother, Danny quickly abandoned school and began playing music to earn money to help his family. According to Danny, his strong grasp of Spanish-language grammar enabled him to rapidly learn English as a second language—one key step he found necessary to earn a living doing business across ethnicities in New York City.

Danny has always been highly motivated to earn money to help support his family. But he feels this is not a simplistic dream of acquiring objects. He also strives to enjoy a more relaxed lifestyle and certain amenities that were not available to him in Ecuador. Danny describes the American Dream as "what you make of it . . . to be doing what I want to do . . . being happy. For me, it's freelancing and doing my music. . . . I could do without half the things I have. People have been sold the idea they need to consume, buy things.

... This is the American Dream. .... I've been in it, the more things you have—the unhappier you are taking all your time to care for these things" (Danny, 2016). Danny believes that a desire for the good life is an acquired Ecuadorian worldview because his fellow countrymen and countrywomen settled in the United States refer to the good life as one of simplicity and contentment. His testimony revealed the symbiotic nature of a good life as an option available to migrants and other historically marginalized individuals sharing the double-consciousness identity. In the spirit of Lok Siu's (2001, 8) definition of cultural citizenship as emphasizing daily "practices of inclusion and exclusion," Danny's homeland norms and values intersect and benefit from his settlement experiences as a successful migrant who practices humanitarianism while exercising personal freedom, and sound judgment.

Danny advocates southern hemisphere cultural solidification through the enhancement of national pride. The artists he promotes appear at immigrant social club events, but Danny does not hold a membership in any of these organizations. In fact, he stressed that he only attends sponsored events for professional reasons. Danny provided his own interpretation of a good life by describing the ways he believes he adheres to the principles of this imagined ideal. "I do this managing of artists and perform myself because it makes me happy to give back to the community. The good life is to leave the politics to the side. A life in which there are no financial worries, and this is not your sole focus. A simple life" (Danny, 2016). Danny's nonpolitical idea of empowerment was not shared by all Ecuadorian migrants developing new empowerment paradigms for immigrant populations. Two case studies demonstrate that a commitment to social and political activism is a common attribute of these new models developed by Ecuadorian migrants to promote a sense of belonging.

Rosie. Social Consciousness and Holistic Environmentalism

Rosie was born in the sierra province of Pichincha, near Quito, in the small town of Barrio Obrero. According to Rosie, hers was like many other middle-class families in Quito. This meant that her father used the rules of Quito's racialized society to closely supervise the hiring of household workers and nannies in accordance with the prevailing dictums of society, which excluded the employment of Afro-Ecuadorians. Rosie described her father as a proud Ecuadorian former member of the Army who exercised complete control to make sure all the bills were paid and there was food on the table. In Ecuador, her mother was not allowed to have anything to do with household financial matters. But when the family migrated to the United States, she became a working housewife. Even before leaving Ecuador, she began to assume a more dominant role, since she initiated the decision to move the family to the United States to seek a better life and greater opportunities. Once the family arrived in their new country, as a more independent woman she slowly convinced her husband to begin to relinquish his total control over the family. In this case, the processes of globalization that sometimes advantaged females in the job market eventually weakened the power of machismo. In contrast, Rosie's maternal grandmother remained in Ecuador, where the unabated practice of male superiority continued to restrict the professional growth of women.

Rosie identifies in Ecuador as mestiza because of her mixed Spanish-Jewish-Indigenous heritage. Her racial-ethnic identity is a matter of pride because she is a dual national of Ecuador and the United States: "I identify myself as North American, because I was raised here [in the United States] and I know the ins and outs. I'm also fully Ecuadorian, I know the culture well, I'm bilingual. In the U.S., I'm White because the only relative that was not White or Spanish was my grandmother" (Rosie, 2016). Rosie feels as though her claim to Whiteness is tempered by her experiences in Los Angeles, a city in which being Latina is often conflated with ideas that racialize all Latin Americans as unworthy Mexicans aliens.

Although her father firmly situated Blacks at the bottom of Ecuador's racial-ethnic social ladder, these narrow ideas about the social stratification of people based on notions of White superiority did not sit well with Rosie. As she entered her last two years in a private Catholic high school in L.A., she found herself at odds with her father's narrow perceptions about the differences in people. Rosie noticed that after his migration her father began to use language that reflected the influence of racialization concepts from both Ecuador and the United States. "I stood up to my father when he disagreed about my wanting to become a bilingual teacher. He said, 'Why are you going to go to work teaching those Mexicans. You teach only English! Why you want to be associated with Mexicans?' He hated being called a Mexican. He thought of them as unsophisticated, uneducated, he was out of touch with César Chávez" (Rosie, 2016).

While in Ecuador for two years after graduating from high school, Rosie followed in the footsteps of her aunt and uncle, who worked with the Indigenous peoples. She watched the middle class of her homeland flaunt their cars and demean their Indigenous maids. The elites shunned the poor, whom they labeled lower class because of their darker skin or their last names that did not appear to sound Spanish or in some way denoted Afro or Indigenous ancestry. During this time away from paternal domination, Rosie lived in the Amazon among the Indigenous, the very people her father had cautioned her to avoid. "I learned about the Ecuador that was of no importance to my father. . . . I learned their culture . . . to care for the land and I learned about poverty" (Rosie, 2016). This time spent in Ecuador marks for Rosie an introduction to the principles of the good life, which she sees as a simple lifestyle based on fairness, compassion, and the production of agency and empowerment.

Rosie returned to the United States and after completing her degree began a career as a bilingual teacher. In this way, she satisfied her father's dream for her to become a professional capable of achieving the American Dream, in spite of his desire for her not to teach bilingual classes. Rosie joined La Liga about two years before our first interview because she was looking for an organization in which her daughter could experience being Ecuadorian. Her plan was for her daughter to learn the customs of her homeland while she developed a relationship with La Liga's members, whom Rosie knew to be well-educated. She felt that being exposed to phonetically correct Spanish spoken by La Liga members would enable and encourage her daughter to speak Spanish clearly and thereby reduce the possibility of her daughter's being misconstrued as a member of the noncitizen lower class in Miami. This rationale implies that Rosie desires to protect her daughter from becoming (as her father would describe it) akin to a Mexican—the conflation of race and class by which noncitizens are represented in Miami.

The participation of Rosie and her daughter at La Liga ended abruptly after they attended only a few events. According to Rosie, her daughter complained that teenagers like herself didn't attend club functions, which appeared to be designed to appeal only to the tastes of an older generation. When asked about La Liga's activities, Rosie responded that she had no idea what projects the club sponsored because "I stopped going and I didn't really notice what they were trying to do" (Rosie, 2016). Rosie, now retired, started her own nonprofit for special-needs children in 2016. Her organization is multicultural and sponsored by Cuban telenovela actor and star William Levy. She describes launching this new venture as a "life-long dream. I now have my family, work, and church responsibilities. The missionary experience in Ecuador—with the Indigenous—turned my world" (Rosie, 2016). In addition to this social consciousness project, Rosie also is involved in nativist and ecological justice initiatives. Her adoption of an Amazonian concern for the environment is embodied in the landscaping at her home and in her community. Rosie's dedication to civil and environmental justice embodies a more active engagement that fits the model of cultural citizenship described by Rosaldo (1997) and Flores and Benmayor (1997). This same deep commitment to promote social justice was shared by José Juan, a more recently arrived Afro-Ecuadorian migrant musician residing in New York City. Anonymous's mantra of "keeping yourself" is a call to action that continues to relate to a new generation of highly skilled migrant workers. Because their transnational migrations are influenced by the forces that shape their double-consciousness identity, the relationships they form inside and outside existing Ecuadorian social clubs will reveal much to future scholars about the process of acculturation.

Conclusion

José Juan. Musical Expression and Cultural Citizenship

José Juan, who now lives in New York City, was born in 1985 in the sierra province of Pichincha. A professional musician prior to migrating in 2006, he trained at the National Conservatory of Music in Quito. While in this prestigious school, he performed as a percussionist throughout North and South America. José describes his family tree as "Super-Afro-Ecuadorian," and in Ecuador he does not claim Indigenous or White ancestry. Self-identifying according to racial and ethnic categories on the U.S. census, José Juan holds a nuanced and contextualized viewpoint about race and space. "Hispano is more about the language. Hispano, we speak Spanish. Hispano is not a race but an understanding of all people who speak Spanish in the Americas" (José Juan, 2015). He felt pride and not resentment that the U.S. census classified him as Latino. "I learned Latinos are doing a hard job in this country. They have given an ultrapositive representation by establishing both a cultural and socioeconomic reputation—more than anything, in this city where I live, Latinos have a lot of feelings about what is going on" (José Juan, 2015).

José Juan's life in Ecuador as a person of African heritage was tainted by racism. His family's three-generation-long legacy as bomba musicians did not protect him from discrimination. José Juan became familiar with the concept of cultural citizenship in the homeland during his tenure in outreach programs at Azúcar, the Afro-Ecuadorian foundation then located in Quito that serves as a guardian of culture and advocate for civil rights. "I had the opportunity to work with Azúcar, and it was one of my first musical endeavors. Azúcar for many years has been trying to liberate us [Afro-Ecuadorians] from oppression. They are working trying to establish our rights not just as Afroecuatorianos but as human beings in our community, yes—our nation." Migration to the United States for José Juan grew out of a need to escape the suffering of structural exclusion and his development of the Chota Madre movement, a mission to "entertain to establish the Afroecuatoriano culture. I'm working to give a future to the music not only in Ecuador but in the world" (José Juan, 2015).

José Juan is a member of a generation of well-educated migrants from Ecuador who are creating new paradigms of empowerment outside Ecuadorian social organizations. In our interview, he spoke about being a part of a transnational movement of workers, revealing his awareness of a disadvantaged double-consciousness identity that is attached to the world's migrant workforce (Wideman, 1990). Unlike traditional Ecuadorian civic clubs, which celebrate cultural pride, José Juan's model has cultural citizenship as its core principle. However, the idea of inclusion for the community served is still heavily influenced by settlement and homeland ideas about racial and ethnic difference.

Network construction for José Juan is primarily with Afro-Latin American friends at work, and his social circle is within the Latino community. His many attempts to reach out to other Ecuadorians in New York, even with homeland migrants of African descent—all ended in rejection. José Juan is a part of the Ecuadorian performers network and, despite his notoriety, he has never participated in the annual ECCNY pageant or parade. Even José Juan admitted that his work schedule limits the amount of time he can devote to his musical mission. Other Ecuadorian migrants in New York I spoke with were unaware that a bomba player of his high caliber lived in their city, evidence that José Juan's mission to make his culture part of the Latin American musical tapestry is a project in its early stages (Figure 12 NYC José Juan Bomba).

Although José Juan's practice of cultural citizenship includes his development of a social consciousness as a Latino, this double-consciousness awareness does not include a universal acceptance of all members of the Black diaspora. He purposefully has few contacts with Afro-Americans, whom he described as suffering from racism in a different way than he experienced in Ecuador. "We [Afro-Ecuadorians] have pride. We think we have to change and work to change life" (José Juan, 2015). According to José Juan, Afro-Americans advancement in society is slow because too many are a part of the drug-based subculture. Also, he feels Afro-Americans accept

Figure 12.
José Juan
Chota Madre
Percussionist

government dependency as normal, and few "know the ways to advance themselves" (José Juan, 2015). Although his cultural citizenship education in Ecuador emphasized the need for global solidarity among members of the African diaspora, his associations as a settler resulted in José Juan's sharing with long-time Ecuadorian migrants a desire to associate himself with successful networks.

José Juan is a professor at Fordham University teaching Afro-Ecuadorian music, and he also goes to school to complete studies in industrial mechanics for the company that sponsored his entry and permanent residency in the United States. "This is my life here, I live to work, to pay debts, to make music. . . . I work a lot to do shows—those shows where I play to build my projects—the music here and the music of Chota Madre are my projects. I play Latin, Latin-Rock, flamenco, there's much music here in New York City by independent artists. My American Dream is to form a pathway for my music in this huge city" (José Juan, 2015). After nine years in the United States living as a person of African heritage, José Juan sees the American Dream as a vehicle that will enable him to bring his family to New York. His idea is not for his family members to acquire wealth. Instead, his hope is that they will have the opportunity to belong in a society that will value them as performing musicians of African heritage. Again, these are ideas that directly correspond to Anonymous's "keeping yourself" principle: the ability to construct and maintain an identity that the individual can believe to be positive and self-propelled.

José Juan's desire for this type of social agency and mobility is a characteristic this study has shown to be shared by Ecuadorian migrants who construct social organizations to foster a sense of belonging in other Latin American migrants.

Belonging is the primary lens employed within this study to analyze the process of Ecuadorian immigration to the United States. Theories from classic Afro-American, Latinx, and feminist scholarship intersect to support the idea that historically repressed multiethnic groups in the United States share a double-consciousness identity with migrant Latin Americans. Throughout this book, the concept of intersectionality has shed light on the oppressiveness of interlacing and sometimes codependent homeland and settlement notions about racial, class, and gender differences. The resulting examination is a synthesis of the construction of success in the three different social climates of Los Angeles, Miami, and New York City. As a work of action in anthropology, this research supports two recommendations to future researchers focusing on immigrant populations. First, topically exploring success as opposed to failure can cast light on the full spectrum of changes that define the merger of homeland and settlement norms, values, and trust. Second, the maligning of Latinx migrants by accusing them of failing to assimilate can be challenged by producing more scholarship about the role of immigrant social clubs and the genesis within them of acculturation.

References

Abascal, M. (2015). Us and them: Black-White relations in the wake of Hispanic population growth. *American Sociological Review, 80*(4), 789–813.

Abramitzky, R., & Boustan, L. (2017). Immigration in American economic history. *Journal of Economic Literature, 55*(4), 1311–1345.

Abrego, L. J. (2014). *Sacrificing families: Navigating laws, labor, and love across borders.* Redwood City, CA: Stanford University Press.

Aja, A. A., Zaw, K., Beesing, G., Price, A. E., Bustillo, D., Darity Jr., W., & Hamilton, D. (2019). *The color of wealth in Miami.* Joint publication of the Kirwan Institute for the Study of Race and Ethnicity at the Ohio State University, the Samuel DuBois Cook Center on Social Equity at Duke University, and the Insight Center for Community Economic Development.

Appadurai, A. (2004). The capacity to aspire: Culture and the terms of recognition. In V. Rao and M. Walton (Eds.), *Culture and public action* (pp. 59–84). Palo Alto, CA: Stanford University Press.

Aranda, E., Chang, R. E., & Sabogal, E. (2016). Racializing Miami, immigrant Latinos and colorblind racism in the global city. In J. A. Cobas, J. Duany, and J. R. Reagin (Eds.), *How the United States racializes Latinos: White hegemony and its consequences* (pp. 149–165). New York: Routledge.

Babis, D. (2016). Understanding diversity in the phenomenon of immigrant organizations: A comprehensive framework. *Journal of International Migration and Integration, 17*(2), 355–369.

Basch, L. (1987). The Vincentians and Grenadians: The role of voluntary associations in immigrant adaptation to New York City. In N. Foner (Ed.), *New immigrants in New York* (pp. 159–193). New York: Columbia University Press.

Basso, K. H. (1996). *Wisdom sits in places: Landscape and language among the Western Apache.* Albuquerque: University of New Mexico Press.

Benavides, O. H. (2004). *Making Ecuadorian histories: Four centuries of defining power.* Austin: University of Texas Press.

Benton, R. A. 2016. Uniters or dividers? Voluntary organizations and social capital acquisition. *Social Networks, 44*, 209–218.

Bertoli, S., Fernández-Huertas Moraga, J., & Ortega, F. (2011). Immigration policies and the Ecuadorian exodus. The World Bank Economic Review, 25(1), 57-76.

Bhabha, H. K. (1994). *The location of culture*. London: Routledge.

Boehm, D. (2016). *Returned: Going and coming in an age of deportation*. Oakland: University of California Press.

Boehm, D. A. (2011). Here/not here: Contingent citizenship and transnational Mexican children. In C. Coe, R. Reynolds, D. A. Boehm, J. M. Hess, and H. Rae-Espinoza (Eds.), *Everyday ruptures: Children, youth, and migration in global perspective* (pp. 161–173). Nashville, TN: Vanderbilt University Press.

Bonilla-Silva, E. (2012). The invisible weight of Whiteness: The racial grammar of everyday life in contemporary America. *Ethnic and Racial Studies, 35*(2), 173–194.

Burridge, A. (2014). "No borders" as a critical politics of mobility and migration. *ACME: An International E-journal for Critical Geographies, 13*(3), 463–470.

Cacho, L. 2012. *Social death: Racialized rightlessness and the criminalization of the unprotected*. New York: New York University Press.

Caro-López, H. (2011). *Ecuadorians in New York City, 1990–2010*. Center for Latin American, Caribbean and Latino Studies (CLACLS) New York City Latino Data Project Series Report, 36(11).

Carter, P. M., & Callesano, S. (2018). The social meaning of Spanish in Miami: Dialect perceptions and implications for socioeconomic class, income, and employment. *Latino Studies, 16*(1), 65–90.

Castañeda, X., & Zavella, P. (2003). Changing constructions of sexuality and risk: Migrant Mexican women farmworkers in California. *Journal of Latin American Anthropology, 8*(2), 126–150.

Chavez, L. R. (2017). *Anchor babies and the challenge of birthright citizenship*. Redwood City, CA: Stanford University Press.

Christopher, S. C., & Leslie, T. F. (2015). Assessing immigrant niches across large American metropolitan areas. *Population, Space and Place, 21*(2), 171–192.

Collins, J. L. (2009).*Threads: Gender, labor, and power in the global apparel industry*. Chicago: University of Chicago Press.

Collins, P. H. (2002). *Black feminist thought: Knowledge, consciousness, and the politics of empowerment* (2nd ed.). New York: Routledge.

Connell, R. W. (1995). *Masculinities* (2nd ed.). Berkeley: University of California Press.

Cordero-Guzmán, H. R. (2005). Community-based organizations and migration in New York City. *Journal of Ethnic and Migration Studies, 31*(5): 889–909.

Crocker, J., & Major, B. (1989). Social stigma and self esteem: The self-protective properties of stigma. *Psychological Review, 96*(4): 608–630.

Davies, C. A. (1998). *Reflexive ethnography: A guide for researching selves and others*. New York: Routledge.

Dawson, A. C. (2014). *In light of Africa: Globalizing Blackness in northeast Brazil*. Toronto: University of Toronto Press.

de la Torre, C. (2010). Social movements and constituent processes in Ecuador. *DEMOCRATIC*, 211–238.

de la Torre, C. (2018). Latin America's shifting politics: Ecuador after Correa. *Journal of Democracy, 29*(4), 77–88.

de la Torre, C., & Conaghan, C. (2009). The hybrid campaign: Tradition and modernity in Ecuador's 2006 presidential election. *International Journal of Press/Politics, 14*, 335–352.

de la Torre, C., & Sánchez, J. A. (2012). The Afro-Ecuadorian social movement. In J. M. Rahier (Ed.), *Black social movements in Latin America: From monocultural mestizaje to multiculturalism* (pp. 135–150). New York: Palgrave Macmillan.

Douglas, M. (1986). *How institutions think*. Syracuse, NY: Syracuse University Press.

Du Bois, W. E. B. (1989). *The souls of Black folk: Authoritative text, contexts, criticism*. Edited by H. L. Gates & H. T. Oliver. New York: Bantam Dell.

Espinosa, A. M., Horna, L., Mendieta Muñoz, R., & Pontarollo, N. (2019). The statistical properties of the networks of emigrants: The Ecuadorian case. *International Migration, 57*(4), 40–57.

Falicov, C. J. (2017). Latino/Latinas in couple and family therapy. In J. Lebow, A. Chambers, & D. C. Breunlin (Eds.), *Encyclopedia of couple and family therapy* (pp. 1–9). New York: Springer.

Fitts, S., & McClure, G. (2015). Building social capital in Hightown: The role of confianza in Latina immigrants' social networks in the New South. *Anthropology & Education Quarterly, 46*(3), 295–311.

Flores, W. F., and Benmayor, R. (1997). "Constructing Cultural Citizenship." In W. F. Flores and R. Benmayor (Eds.), *Latino cultural citizenship: Claiming identity, space, and rights* (pp. 255-277). Boston: Beacon.

Foner, N. (2001). Transnationalism then and now: New York immigrants today and at the turn of the twentieth century. In H. R. Cordero-Guzmán, R. C. Smith, & R. Grosfoguel (Eds.), *Migration, transnationalization, and race in a changing New York* (pp. 35–57). Philadelphia: Temple University Press.

Fox, M., Thayer, Z. M., & Wadhwa, P. D. (2017). Acculturation and health: The moderating role of sociocultural context. *American Anthropologist, 119*(3), 405–421.

Galván, R. T., & La Vereda, G. U. (2006). *Campesina* epistemologies and pedagogies of the spirit: Examining women's *sobrevivencia*. In D. D.

Bernal, C. A. Elenes, F. E. Godinez, & S. Villenas (Eds.), *Chicana/Latina education in everyday life: Feminista perspectives on pedagogy and epistemology* (pp. 161–179). Albany: State University of New York Press.

Gilmore, R. W. (2007). *Golden gulag: Prisons, surplus, crisis, and opposition in globalizing California.* Berkeley: University of California Press.

Gilroy, P. (1993). The Black Atlantic as a counterculture of modernity. In *The Black Atlantic: Modernity and double consciousness* (pp. 1–40). Cambridge, MA: Harvard University Press.

Golash-Boza, T. (2015). *Immigration nation: Raids, detentions, and deportations in post-9/11 America.* New York: Pilgrim.

Gosin, M. (2019). *The racial politics of division: Interethnic struggles for legitimacy in multicultural Miami.* Ithaca, NY: Cornell University Press.

Gratton, B. (2007). Ecuadorians in the United States and Spain: History, gender and niche formation. *Journal of Ethnic and Migration Studies, 33*(4), 581–599.

Grenier, G. J., & Stepick, A., III. (1992). *Miami now! Immigration, ethnicity, and social change.* Gainesville: University Press of Florida.

Gutmann, M., & Viveros, M. (2004). Masculinities in Latin America. In M. S. Kimmel, J. Hearn, & R. W. Connell (Eds.), *Handbook of studies on men and masculinities* (pp. 114–128). Thousand Oaks, CA: Sage.

Hansberry, L. (1959). *A raisin in the sun.* London: Samuel French.

Harrison, F. V. (2002). Global apartheid, foreign policy, and human rights. *Souls, 4*(3), 48–68.

Hein, J. (1995). *From Vietnam, Laos, and Cambodia: A refugee experience in the United States.* New York: Twayne.

Hollenstein, P. (2009). La reproducción de la dominación racial: Las experiencias de una familia indígena en Quito. Quito: FLACSO.

Jefferson, A. (2015). Not what it used to be: Schemas of class and contradiction in the Great Recession. *Economic Anthropology, 2*(2): 310–325.

Johnson, G. T. (2013). *Spaces of conflict, sounds of solidarity: Music, race, and spatial entitlement in Los Angeles.* Berkeley: University of California Press.

Jokisch, B. D., & Kyle, D. (2008). Ecuadorian international migration. In C. de la Torre and S. Striffler (Eds.), *The Ecuador reader: History, culture, politics* (pp. 350–358). Durham, NC: Duke University Press.

Joseph, T. D. (2015). *Race on the move: Brazilian migrants and the global reconstruction of race.* Redwood City, CA: Stanford University Press.

Jütersonke, O., Muggah, R., & Rodgers, D. (2009). Gangs, urban violence, and security interventions in Central America. *Security Dialogue, 40*(4–5), 373–397.

Kearney, M. (1995). The local and the global: The anthropology of globalization and transnationalism. *Annual Review of Anthropology, 24,* 547–565.

Lambek, M. (2010). Introduction. In M. Lambek (Ed.), *Ordinary ethics: Anthropology, language, and action* (pp. 1–36). New York: Fordham University Press.

Lamphere, L. (1992). *Structuring diversity: Ethnographic perspectives on the new immigration.* Chicago: University of Chicago Press.

Lee, S. S. (2014). *Building a Latino civil rights movement: Puerto Ricans, African Americans, and the pursuit of racial justice in New York City.* Chapel Hill: University of North Carolina Press.

Levitt, P. (2003). Keeping feet in both worlds: Transnational practices and immigrant incorporation in the United States. In C. Joppke & E. Morawska, *Integrating immigrants in liberal nation-states: Policies and practices* (pp. 177–94). New York: Springer.

López, G. (2015). "Hispanics of Mexican origin in the United States, 2013." Washington, DC: Pew Research Center.

Loukaitou-Sideris, A., & Hutchinson, J. (2006). Social networks and social capital Latinos in Pico-Union. In P. Ong and A. Loukaitou-Sideris (Eds.), *Jobs and economic development in minority communities* (pp. 235–256). Philadelphia: Temple University Press.

Low, S. (2016). *Spatializing culture: The ethnography of space and place.* New York: Routledge.

Low, S. M. (2009). Towards an anthropological theory of space and place. *Semiotica, 175,* 21–37.

Mancheno, K. M. (2010). Ecuador: Efectos de la emigración en los resultados educativos. *Historia Actual Online, 22,* 57–75.

Marcus, G. E. (1995). Ethnography in and of the world system: The emergence of multi-sited ethnography. *Annual Review of Anthropology, 24,* 95–117.

Marshall, T. H. (1950). *Citizenship and social class, and other essays.* Cambridge: Cambridge University Press.

McNamee, S. J., & Miller, R. K. (2009). *The meritocracy myth* (2nd ed.). Lanham, MD: Rowman & Littlefield.

Mayorga-Gallo, S., & Hordge-Freeman, E. (2017). Between marginality and privilege: Gaining access and navigating the field in multiethnic settings. *Qualitative Research, 17*(4), 377–394.

Meyrowitz, J. (1985). *No sense of place: The impact of electronic media on social behavior.* Oxford: Oxford University Press.

Miles, A. (2004). *From Cuenca to Queens: An anthropological story of transnational migration.* Austin: University of Texas Press.

Minian, A. R. (2018). *Undocumented lives: The untold story of Mexican migration*. Cambridge, MA: Harvard University Press..

Ngai, M. M. (2014). *Impossible subjects: Illegal aliens and the making of modern America, updated edition*. Princeton, NJ: Princeton University Press.

Nobles, W. W. (1974). Africanity: Its role in Black families. *Black Scholar*, 5(9), 10–17.

Novo, C. M. (2009). *Repensando los movimientos indígenas*. Quito: FLACSO-Sede Ecuador.

O'Connor, C. (2017). Embodiment and the construction of social knowledge: Towards an integration of embodiment and social representations theory. *Journal for the Theory of Social Behaviour*, 47(1), 2–24.

Ortner, S. B. 2016. Dark anthropology and its others: Theory since the eighties. *HAU: Journal of Ethnographic Theory*, 6(1), 47–73.

Paz-y-Miño, C., Guillen Sacoto, M. J., and Leone, P. E. (2016). Genetics and genomic medicine in Ecuador. *Molecular Genetics & Genomic Medicine*, 4(1): 9–17.

Portes, A. (1998). Social capital: Its origins and applications in modern sociology. *Annual Review of Sociology*, 24(1), 1–24.

Portes, A., & Bach, R. L. (1985). *Latin journey: Cuban and Mexican immigrants in the United States*. Berkeley: University of California Press.

Portes, A., Escobar, C., & Walton Radford, A. (2007). Immigrant transnational organizations and development: A comparative study. *International Migration Review*, 41(1), 242–281.

Pribilsky, J. (2007). *La chulla vida: Gender, migration, and the family in Andean Ecuador and New York City*. Syracuse, NY: Syracuse University Press.

Rahier, J. M. (2008). Soccer and the (tri-)color of the Ecuadorian nation: Visual and ideological (dis-)continuities of Black otherness from monocultural mestizaje to multiculturalism. *Visual Anthropology Review*, 24(2), 148–182.

Rapport, N., & Overing, J. 2000. *Social and cultural anthropology: The key concepts*. London: Routledge.

Reed-Danahay, D., Brettell, C. B., et al. (2008). *Citizenship, political engagement, and belonging: Immigrants in Europe and the United States*. New Brunswick, NJ: Rutgers University Press.

Rodseth, L. (2018). Hegemonic concepts of culture: The checkered history of dark anthropology. *American Anthropologist*, 120(3), 398–411.

Roitman, K. (2008). Hybridity, *mestizaje*, and *montubios* in Ecuador. QEH Working Paper Series, 165, 1–19.

Rosaldo, R. (1997). Cultural citizenship, inequality, and multiculturalism. In W. F. Flores and R. Benmayor (Eds.), *Latino cultural citizenship: Claiming identity, space, and rights* (pp. 205-219). Boston: Beacon, 1997.

Rose, C. N. (2015). *The struggle for Black freedom in Miami: Civil rights and America's tourist paradise, 1896-1968*. Baton Rouge: Louisiana State University Press.

Ruby, J. (Ed.). (1982). *A crack in the mirror: Reflexive perspectives in anthropology*. Philadelphia: University of Pennsylvania Press.

Rumbaut, R. G., and Portes, A. (2001). *Ethnicities: Children of immigrants in America*. Berkeley: University of California Press.

Sahlins, M. (2013). *Culture and practical reason*. Chicago: University of Chicago Press.

Sánchez, J. A. (2013). Afrodescendencia, participación política y proceso electoral 2013. *Democracias*, 1, 149-214.

Sanjek, R. (2000). *The future of us all: Race and neighborhood politics in New York City*. Ithaca, NY: Cornell University Press.

Schensul, J. J., & LeCompte, M. D. (2016). *Ethnography in action: A mixed methods approach* (Vol. 7). Lanham, MD: Rowman & Littlefield.

Scholte, B. (1981). Critical anthropology since its reinvention. In J. Kahn (Ed.), *The anthropology of pre-capitalist societies* (pp. 148-184). London: Macmillan.

Siu, L. C. (2001). Diasporic cultural citizenship: Chineseness and belonging in Central America. *Social Text*, 19(4), 7-28.

Smedley, A. (1998). Race and the construction of human identity. *American Anthropologist*, 100(3), 690-702.

Sonenshein, R. J. (2013). *The city at stake: Secession, reform, and the battle for Los Angeles*. Princeton, NJ: Princeton University Press.

Spears, A. K., & Hinton, L. (2010). Languages and speakers: An introduction to African American English and Native American languages. *Transforming Anthropology*, 18(1), 3-14.

Stoll, D. (2009). Which American dream do you mean? *Society*, 46(5), pp. 398-402.

Strawn, K. D. (2009). Contemporary research on social movements and protest in Latin America: Promoting democracy, resisting neoliberalism, and many themes in between. *Sociology Compass*, 3(4), 644-657.

Vertovec, S. (2009). *Transnationalism*. New York: Routledge.

Wideman, J. E. (1990). Introduction. In W. E. B. Du Bois, *The souls of Black folk* (pp. xiii). New York: Random House.

Wilson, W. J. (1987). *The truly disadvantaged*. Chicago: University of Chicago Press.

Wyly, E., Newman, K., Schafran, A., & Lee, E. (2010). Displacing New York. *Environment and Planning A, 42*(11), 2602-2623.

Yuval-Davis, N. (2006). Belonging and the politics of belonging. *Patterns of prejudice, 40*(3), 197-214.

Zambrana, R. E., & Zoppi, I. M. (2002). Latina students: Translating cultural wealth into social capital to improve academic success. *Journal of Ethnic and Cultural Diversity in Social Work, 11*(1-2), 33-53.

Zentella, A. C. (1997). *Growing up bilingual: Puerto Rican children in New York.* Malden, MA: Blackwell.

Zhou, M., & Lee, R. (2013). Transnationalism and community building: Chinese immigrant organizations in the United States. *Annals of the American Academy of Political and Social Science, 647*(1), 22-49.

CPSIA information can be obtained
at www.ICGtesting.com
Printed in the USA
LVHW040725230523
747759LV00001B/193